Eva Philipps

Documentation Made Easy

A Library Manual for Nongovernmental Organizations
Specializing in Appropriate Technology and Rural
Development

A Publication of
Deutsches Zentrum für Entwicklungstechnologien – GATE
in: Deutsche Gesellschaft für Technische Zusammenarbeit (GTZ) GmbH

Friedr. Vieweg & Sohn   Braunschweig/Wiesbaden

The author:
Eva Philipps, graduate librarian. After having been employed for several years in the Federal Republic of Germany, during which she set up libraries at various organizations, Ms. Philipps worked as a consultant in Indonesia from 1971 – 1973. This was followed by several short-term assignments as a consultant in the setting up of small libraries in the Yemen Arab Republic, Kenya and Indonesia. Since then she has worked on a free-lance basis with GATE/GTZ in the field of documentation, and has done NGO work in Southeast Asia.

Drawings: Dorsi German

Deutsche Bibliothek Cataloguing-in-Publication Data

Philipps, Eva:
Documentation made easy : a library manual for
nongovernmental organizations specializing in appropriate
technology and rural development / Eva Philipps. A publ. of
Dt. Zentrum für Entwicklungstechnologien – GATE in: Dt.
Ges. für Techn. Zusammenarbeit (GTZ) GmbH. –
Braunschweig ; Wiesbaden : Vieweg, 1990
  ISBN 3-528-02054-7

The author's opinion does not necessarily represent the view of the publisher.

Published by Friedr. Vieweg & Sohn Verlagsgesellschaft mbH, Braunschweig
Vieweg is a subsidiary company of the Bertelsmann Publishing Group International.

Printed in the Federal Republic of Germany by Lengericher Handelsdruckerei, Lengerich

ISBN 3-528-02054-7

Contents

Preface

This manual has been written to help those who are faced with the task of setting up a small library/documentation centre or who are already working in such a centre, without having learned basic documentation techniques. In particular, it has been developed in response to the needs of non-governmental organizations (NGOs) in the Third World, working in the field of appropriate technology (AT) and rural development, with a need for information in a processed form for their daily work.

Some people will ask why it is necessary to produce yet another library/documentation manual. Most manuals I have come across are too sophisticated, often assuming that the reader is already familiar with basic techniques such as cataloguing. This manual is aimed at non-librarians, i.e. those who have had no formal training in documentation work but who have been assigned to do the library job in their organization — be it in their role as secretary, accountant, engineer or social scientist. It has been written for those who have no access to short-term training courses on library/documentation techniques; for those who do not have the time to study voluminous textbooks on cataloguing and classification and who do not yet have the experience to decide which rules are basic and which ones can be ignored by smaller libraries.

In comparison to other currently available manuals on information science and documentation techniques, this guide is very short which is an indication that it is far from complete. It is intended to convey only those basic techniques which the careful reader will be able to use as a starting point. More detailed textbooks should be consulted (a list of books suggested for further reading is provided at the back) for answers to more specific questions.

One initial decision is the naming of the service or facility that you are establishing. Various terms are currently in use, such as "library", "documentation centre", "documentation unit", "information centre" or simply "documentation". Although there is a defined difference between 'library' and 'documentation centre', the terms are nevertheless used in an almost interchangeable way. I personally think that it does not really matter which descriptive term is used — what matters is the quality of the service offered. Since the average nongovernmental organization or even small governmental organization will have to handle a great variety of publications, it might as well be called a library as a documentation centre.

Some people doubt the necessity to organize and manage a small library/documentation centre according to internationally accepted rules. They think it sufficient to shelve the books according to order and that card catalogues are not necessary. They are right as long as the collection does not exceed a total number of approximately 500 copies/entries. Within this range it is still possible to remember the available books and documents and to search for them without losing too much time. But if the collection grows and/or a change of personnel occurs — as is so often the case in small NGO libraries —, it becomes more and more difficult or even impossible to retrieve the information needed within a reasonable period of time. You never know beforehand whether and to what extent your library will grow in the future. Therefore, it is advisable to set up even a very small library according to basic international standards as far as cataloguing and classification systems are concerned. These standards will guarantee that any future expansion of the library can be carried out without having to change the whole system.

You may wonder why there is no chapter in this manual on the use of computers in information processing. There are various reasons for this:

(a) For a small library computerized information processing is not necessary — even if the collection is expected to grow considerably (10,000 to 15,000 volumes) in the next 5 – 10 years.

(b) Many people think that computers do the job by themselves and they forget or do not know that a tremendous input of time and know-how is needed before a system works satisfactorily.

(c) Even if you are considering using a computer for information processing, basic documentation techniques as described here are indispensable.

(d) Although personal computers are already being used by many NGOs in the Third World for word processing and accounting, they are not yet used frequently for data processing because larger storage capacities and specially designed software programs are needed.

8

(e) Organizations which have decided to computerize information processing will already have the manuals accompanying the respective software program, for example the CDS/ISIS (UNESCO) program.

It is assumed that the distribution of this English-language version of the manual will be largest in Asia. That is why most of the examples have been taken from the Asian region (names, institutions, etc.). But this does not imply that the manual is not meant for AT NGOs in other parts of the world. Any other English-speaking organization may, of course, use it. In case an organization, active in a country where English is not predominant, wishes to use the manual some parts (particularly abbreviations) may have to be adapted to the language in use.

I am very grateful to Mrs. Nancy Rajczak, chief librarian at the Amerika-Haus (USIS) in Frankfurt/Main, Federal Republic of Germany, for her valuable suggestions regarding language and content. I also would like to thank the staff members of GATE's information unit (Wolfgang Barina, Klaus Wiesner and Helma Zeh-Gasser) who took the time and effort to check the Rural Development Classification (RDC) Model and made many useful suggestions for its improvement. Last but not least I would like to point out that the idea behind this manual is based on the many questions asked by librarians whom I have advised during short-term assignments and by other friends in Southeast Asia. Thanks to Delia, Otje, Mulupi, Mohammed, Mansoor, Sunil and Philip.

During the "Training Course on Basic Documentation Techniques" held in cooperation with GATE's partner institution SIBAT in the Philippines between November 14 and December 3, 1988 the manual underwent a practical test. I would like to say thank you to all participants of the training course for taking the trouble to test the manual.

I hope the readers of this manual will be successful in carrying out their important task. If you have any further questions, please do not hesitate to write to GATE (GATE, Question-and-Answer Service, P.O.Box 5180, D-6236 Eschborn 1, Federal Republic of Germany) for further advice.

Eva Philipps

Abbreviations

AACR	Anglo-American Cataloging Rules
acc. no.	accession number
AT	Appropriate Technology
b/w	black and white
bibliogr.	bibliography
col.	colour
comp.	compiled
Comp.	compiler
DDC	Dewey Decimal Classification
Ed.	editor
ed.	edited
enl.	enlarged
et al.	and others
fig.	figure
GATE	German Appropriate Technology Exchange
ill.	illustrated/illustration
LC	Library of Congress
NGO	nongovernmental organization
no.	number
nos.	numbers
p.	page
RDC	Rural Development Classification
ref.	reference
rev.	revised
SATIS	Socially Appropriate Technology International Information Services
sd.	sound
Transl.	translator
transl.	translated
UDC	Universal Decimal Classification
vol. or v.	volume

1. How to Start

Here you are — surrounded by piles of books and documents and you do not know what to do with them although you have just been appointed the new librarian/documentalist of your organization. You know that these books have to be put into order — but which system will be best and not too difficult to achieve? You do not even know where and how to start.

This manual aims at helping you to carry out your seemingly impossible task. We are quite confident that you will find after having studied the manual that it is not as difficult as you may have feared.

So let us start together from the very beginning. Besides books and documents you will, of course, need a separate library room with basic furniture and equipment. If your organization cannot provide a separate room for the library — this may be the case if all of you are working together in one open-plan office — it is advisable to separate a part of the office with shelves and/or desks and tables. (A detailed description of how to furnish and equip a library can be found in Chapter 14.)

The first step in setting up your library should be to roughly sort the available books and documents according to main subjects. The main subjects should be in accordance with the main tasks of your organization. If you already know which classification scheme you are going to use, you should, of course, use the main groups of that system. Otherwise, you could use the following preliminary groups for sorting:

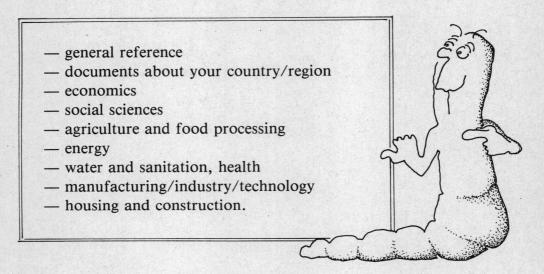

— general reference
— documents about your country/region
— economics
— social sciences
— agriculture and food processing
— energy
— water and sanitation, health
— manufacturing/industry/technology
— housing and construction.

The shelves should be labelled accordingly. You then take one book at a time, briefly check its contents and put it on the appropriate shelf. Thus, potential users can already have partial access to library materials. This is also a preliminary step in classification of the books which will be done later (see Chapters 4 + 5).

All journals and magazines should also first be put together on one shelf even if they deal with different subjects.

One shelf should be reserved for all those books and documents the subject of which you are not yet sure. Now your library is starting to look like a library although it is still just a collection of books.

While roughly sorting the books you should also weed out the ones which are useless and not relevant to your library. It is pointless to keep books and documents that no-one will probably ever read. A documentation centre, for instance, specializing in agriculture will not need a student's textbook on medicine. And it does not make sense to keep a German-language book if none of the library users can read German. Such books are to be discarded. See also Chapter 8 "Foreign Language Books" and Chapter 12 "Acquisition".

The next step is to enter all publications (excluding the journals) in the accessions book.

Before going on we would like to introduce the book which will serve as an example for cataloguing and classifying throughout this manual (see Fig. 1). With this example we will show you step by step how the catalogue card will be completed. The striped bookworm will guide you through the manual and point out our example as it develops. The plain bookworm will point out sentences to be remembered and also key rules.

Fig. 1: The "bookworm" example (page 15 – 21) ▶

Herbert Bergmann

Primary School Agriculture
Vol. I: Pedagogy

Published by Friedr. Vieweg & Sohn Verlagsgesellschaft mbH, Braunschweig
Printed in the Federal Republic of Germany by Lengericher Handelsdruckerei, Lengerich

ISBN 3-528-02013-X
back of the title page

A Publication of
Deutsches Zentrum für Entwicklungstechnologien – GATE
and Division 22 – Education, Science and Universities, Sports
in: Deutsche Gesellschaft für Technische Zusammenarbeit (GTZ) GmbH

Friedr. Vieweg & Sohn   Braunschweig/Wiesbaden

Contents (Volume I: Pedagogy)

our example

16

Herbert Bergmann/Richard Butler

Primary School Agriculture
Vol. II: Background Information

CIP-Kurztitelaufnahme der Deutschen Bibliothek

Bergmann, Herbert:
Primary school agriculture : a publ. of Dt. ⟨...⟩
für Entwicklungstechnologien – GATE and D⟨...⟩
22 – Education, Science and Univ., Sports in: L⟨...⟩
Ges. für Techn. Zusammenarbeit (GTZ) GmbH /
Bergmann ; Richard Butler. – Braunschweig ;
Wiesbaden : Vieweg·
   Vol. 1 verf. von Herbert Bergmann
NE: Butler, Richard:
Vol. 2. Background information. – 1985.
   ISBN 3-528-02014-8

Our example

*back of the
   title page*

Published by Friedr. Vieweg & Sohn Verlagsgesellschaft mbH, Braunschweig
Printed in the Federal Republic of Germany by Lengericher Handelsdruckerei, Lengerich

ISBN 3-528-02014-8

A Publication of
Deutsches Zentrum für Entwicklungstechnologien – GATE
and Division 22 – Education, Science and Universities, Sports
in: Deutsche Gesellschaft für Technische Zusammenarbeit (GTZ) GmbH

V

Friedr. Vieweg & Sohn   Braunschweig/Wiesbaden

Contents (Vol. II: Background Information)

Part II: Crops

Part III: Crop Storage

21

2. Accessions Book/Accession Number

All books, documents, studies, reports, etc., should be listed in an accessions book upon receipt. If you are just starting your library/documentation centre, you should list the existing books as the first step in the cataloguing process. Each book will receive an individual number — the accession number. The accession number is composed of the year of purchase (or the year you started your library) and the current number within that year, for instance 87:105 refers to the 105th book received in 1987. The first book received in 1988 will the number 88:1.

The accession number identifies each book in your library and is particularly useful in distinguishing between multiple copies or different volumes of one title. If, for instance, the two available copies of the Liklik Buk Manual have been borrowed and one is returned by mail without mentioning the borrower's name, you can only find out which copy was returned by comparing the accession number in the book with the one on the lending slip.

The accessions book also serves statistical purposes. At any given time you will be able to tell how many books/documents are in the library or, for example, how many new books have been received between January and October 1987. In addition, if an important book is lost or has been stolen (which sometimes happens!) and an additional copy must be ordered, you can find out where you originally obtained it (the supplier) and the price you paid by looking up the book's accession number in the accessions book. In the accessions book, the following basic data on a publication will be listed:

— accession number
— date of purchase/entry
— author
— title (if necessary in an abridged form)
— supplier (bookseller, supplying organization, donor)
— price
— remarks.

Accession number	Date	Author	Titel	supplier	price	Remarks
87:65	7.9.	Aprovecho	Fuel-saving Cook stoves	GATE	free	
87:66	10.9.	Grace	Cassava proces. sing	FAO	US$ 5.25	
87:67	10.9.	—	Oxford Dictionary	bookshop	Rs 150,-	
87:68	20.9.	Bergmann	Primary School Agriculture. Vol 1	GATE	free	
87:69	20.9	Bergmann	" • Vol. 2	GATE	free	

Fig. 2: Accessions book

Do not waste time searching for details which cannot be easily found.
Leave those columns blank.

The form of the accessions book should be as shown in Fig. 2.

After having entered the book in the accessions book, you should stamp
the title page with the library stamp and write the accession number in its
proper place.

The library stamp should have approximately the form and size indicated
below. If possible, not only the name of the organization but also the

Fig. 3: Library/ownership stamp

address should be given — it improves the chances that books will be returned! The call number will be filled in after the main class number of the book has been determined (see also Chapters 4 and 11.2).

Now the book is ready for cataloguing!

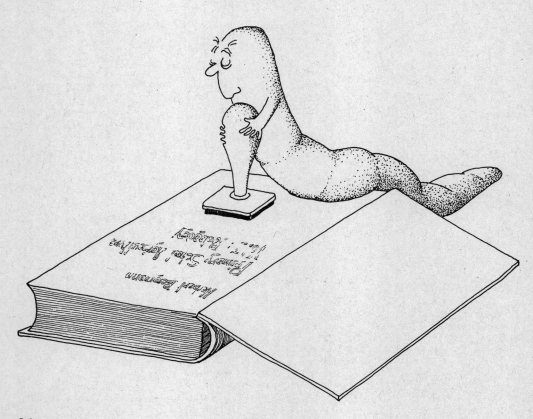

3. Cataloguing or Bibliographic Description

Transferring information about a book/document to a card according to set rules is called cataloguing. There are many international and national cataloguing conventions. The most widespread are the "Anglo-American Cataloging Rules (AACR)" to which this manual refers from time to time. These rules deal with all kinds of questions a cataloguer in large libraries might be faced with. And there are hundreds of rules and exceptions! You will be familiar with the proverb "The exception proves the rule". We do not think it is necessary for a small library to follow all these detailed rules by the letter. **However it is necessary to know the basic rules and to stick to them since UNIFORMITY IS THE MOST IMPORTANT PRINCIPLE IN A LIBRARY!** A book or docu-

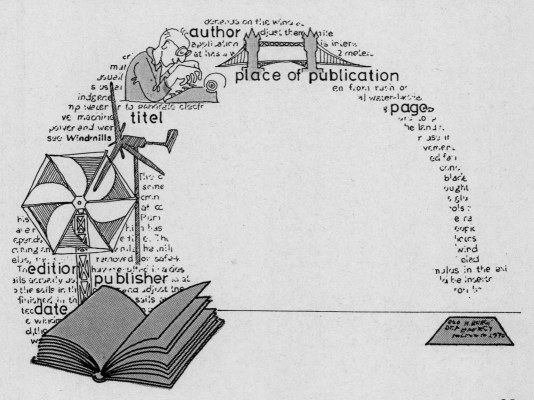

ment not catalogued according to the rules formulated for your library can very easily be lost, i.e. it cannot be retrieved in the catalogues. It is for instance absolutely necessary that a user can rely on the rule that the main heading of a publication will always be the author (unless the publication does not have an author).

Cataloguing can also be defined as the description of a work by its essential characteristics. Such essential elements are:

- o AUTHOR
- o TITLE AND SUBTITLE
- o NUMBER OF VOLUMES
- o EDITION
- o PLACE OF PUBLICATION
- o PUBLISHER
- o DATE OF PUBLICATION
- o NUMBER OF PAGES, ILLUSTRATIONS, APPENDICES, TABLES, FIGURES
- o SERIES

Because a book can be identified by these elements, the catalogue card to which these elements will be transferred and which gives all the information necessary for the complete identification of a work is called the **identity card**. Since this entry also contains information on all other headings under which the work is entered in the catalogue it is also called the **main entry card.** Its other name is **unit card,** i.e. the basic catalogue card which when duplicated may be used as a unit for all other entries.

You may ask yourself why it is necessary to prepare catalogue cards, why it is not sufficient to simply put books into order on the shelves. If your collection does not exceed a maximum of 500 volumes, you actually do not need catalogue cards (and then you do not have to go on reading this manual!) since the average human brain is capable of remembering this amount of information. But if your collection is larger and/or expected to grow considerably, you should start cataloguing the books as eventually you will realize that it is impossible to recall all available books and their contents. So catalogue cards serve to aid the memory of the librarian and the library user!

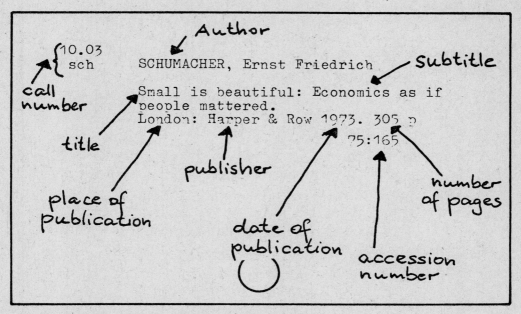

Fig. 4: Main entry card/unit card/identity card

How does one identify the above mentioned elements? The answer is extremely simple: Just read! But you must read a book in a different way from what you are probably used to. Presumably you have read until now for information or entertainment only. In order to do your new job well you should learn how to read a book technically. As a cataloguer you should train yourself to recognize quickly certain characteristics peculiar to books in general and to identify them in each book you handle. The advantage of reading a book in such a way is that you can quickly determine what the book is about and can pass this information on to library users. When you pick up a book you should first look at the title page and the back of the title page. The title page need not be identical with the book cover or cover page but it can be. Sometimes the title is printed on the book cover in an abbreviated form and the subtitle is not mentioned at all. Other important sources of information about the book are the table of contents, the preface, and the index.

Before going on to describe the essential elements of a publication some technical hints should be given. For a beginner in cataloguing, it is advisable to first write a rough copy of the entry by hand on jotting paper about the size of the catalogue cards (also called 'work slip'). When you are more experienced and if you are typing the cards yourself, it is sufficient to only note the most important elements by hand. (For more information see Chapter 10 ''Preparation and Reproduction of Catalogue Cards''.) If you do not do the typing yourself, it is of course necessary to prepare a draft in legible handwriting so that the typist will be able to type the cards correctly. But no matter how legible your handwriting, always put the manuscript catalogue card into the respective book. While doing the final typing a cross-check of the manuscript with the printed information in the book may be useful and necessary.

But now let's start with the real cataloguing!

The first element you should look for is the author.

3.1 Author

''By 'author' is meant the person or corporate body chiefly responsible for the creation of the intellectual or artistic content of a work. The term 'author' also embraces an editor or compiler who has primary responsi-

28

bility for the content of a work, e.g. the compiler of a bibliography.'' (Definition by the Anglo-American Cataloging Rules <AACR>). The author's name is used as the main heading except for anonymous books and documents for which the title is used as heading.

3.1.1 Personal Author

A book may have been written by one, two or more persons. When there are one, two or three names mentioned on the title page all are indicated on the main entry card and by doing so they can be retrieved in the author catalogue (see also Chapter 3.8 ''Added Entries''). When there are more than three authors only the first author is indicated followed by ''et al.'' (this means ''and others'' in Latin; it is the officially used abbreviation). The surname/family name has always to be written first, for example SCHUMACHER, Ernst Friedrich.

The surname should be typed in capital letters in order to enable the user to immediately identify the main heading. The surname is followed by the Christian/given name(s), separated by a comma.

Surnames with Separately Written Prefixes[1]

"Enter a surname that includes a separately written prefix consisting of an article, a preposition, or a combination of the two, under the element most commonly used as entry element in alphabetical listings in the person's language." <AACR> Such prefixes can be "de", "van", "van der", "von", "la" and "Mac". They are part of the surname and that is why they have to be mentioned on the catalogue card. Since these prefixes are quite common in some European languages, most European libraries ignore them as entry criteria as it would be confusing for the user and the librarian to have many entries in the author catalogue starting, for instance, with 'van' and 'von'. Therefore we suggest entering such names under their most distinctive element and according to the prevalent practices in your own country.

Examples for Surnames with Separately Written Prefixes

Dutch/Flemish names:	A. van Gelder = GELDER, A. van
	Menno ter Braak = BRAAK, Menno ter
	Leo op de Bleech = BLEECH, Leo op de
French name:	G. de Lepeleire = LEPELEIRE, G. de
German name:	Hilda von Krosigk = KROSIGK, Hilda von
Italian name:	Edoardo di Muro = MURO, Edoardo di
Spanish name:	D.B. de Padua = PADUA, D.B. de
Swedish name:	Gunnar af Hallstrom = HALLSTROM, Gunnar af

Exception 1: Since "Mac" and "Mc" are regarded as integral parts of the name these prefixes will always be written first, for example:
J.D. Mac Kenzie = MACKENZIE, J.D.
Warwick McKean = MCKEAN, Warwick

Exception 2: If the prefix is not written separately but combined with the name you should enter the name under the prefix, for example:
Lane deMoll = DEMOLL, Lane

---

[1] For more detailed information see also Annex II.

```
ABDUL HAKIM
SCHUMACHER , Ernst
van der    von MAC
op de      LI Fan
       MWANGI,M
     BARAKAT
    MACHFUS
Leo op
Menno
van der
D.B.de
DEMOLL

AIDOO,
Ama A.
```

Names in Various Languages

Sometimes it is difficult to ascertain which part of the name is in fact the surname, as rules vary in different languages. In most languages it is the last name. But in **Spanish,** for instance, it quite often is the middle name. Example: Gabriel Garcia Marquez = GARCIA Marquez, Gabriel

Julio Valladolid Rivera = VALLADOLID Rivera, Julio

But there is also the case of the Indian name K. Krishna Prasad. According to bibliographies the surname is KRISHNA PRASAD, K. and not PRASAD, K. Krishna.

In **Chinese** the first part of the name is regarded as the surname unless the name consists of a Western given name and a Chinese family name:

Examples: Li Fan Quiang   = LI Fan Quiang
           Zhang Wei   = ZHANG Wei
           Richard Lee   = LEE, Richard

31

African names

In most African countries the last part of the name is regarded as the family name.

Examples: Ama Ata Aidoo = AIDOO, Ama Ata
           Meja Mwangi   = MWANGI, Meja

But in some countries the first name is the more significant element. The name is then entered exactly as it appears on the title page (see also Annex II).

Arabic names

When an Arabic name has only two elements, the second element is the surname.

Examples: Nagib Machfus = MACHFUS, Nagib
           Fatimah Barakat = BARAKAT, Fatimah

The prefixes Al, El, Abou, Abun, Abdul, Abdel, Ben, and Ibn are the first element of a compound name.

Examples: Tahir Abdul Hakim = ABDUL HAKIM, Tahir
           Mohammed Al-Afghani = AL-AFGHANI, Mohammed

AUTHOR'S PERSONAL REMARK :

Please don't let this subject drive you mad! Usually it is sufficient to use your common sense. Sometimes even the publisher and editor do not master all these rules and therefore make mistakes! But once you decide how compound names are to be treated in your library, you should adhere to that decision and make a note of it. When a similar case comes up, you can look up your notes and catalogue according to your rules and how you have done it before.

Actually, there is no internationally recognized rule on how to treat prefixes — library practices vary from language to language. Sometimes it is helpful to check how a name is treated in bibliographies or lists of references. And you will certainly know how to treat the names common in your own culture!

Titles and Academic Degrees

No mention should be made of titles and academic degrees such as Sir, Datuk, Bapak, Prof., Sister, Dr., Ph.D., M.A., Father, Engineer, etc. Even if they are indicated on the title page, you should ignore them on the entry card.

No mention is made either of positions such as "President" or "XYZ staff member". At least on catalogue cards, all men are equal!

Second and Third Authors

The second and third authors should also be indicated on the entry card following the title and subtitle (see Figs. 5, 6). The three dots which follow "By" stand for the first author's name. It is not necessary to repeat his name.

Fig. 5: Cataloguing example: first and second authors

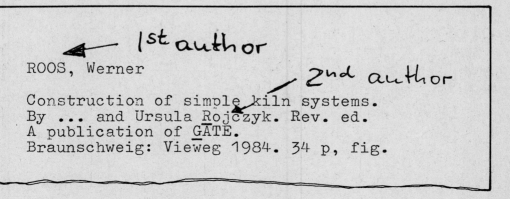

ROOS, Werner

Construction of simple kiln systems.
By ... and Ursula Rojczyk. Rev. ed.
A publication of GATE.
Braunschweig: Vieweg 1984. 34 p, fig.

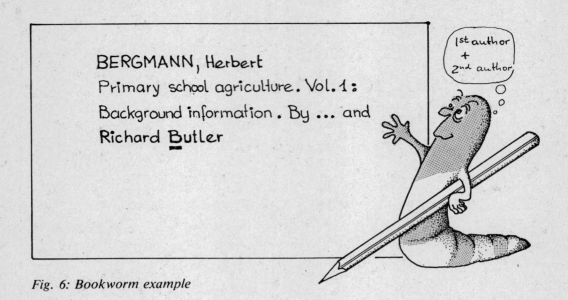

Fig. 6: Bookworm example

More than Three Authors

If a work has been composed by four or more authors and no mention is made of an editor the main heading will be the title. But the first author will be indicated on the entry card (see Fig. 7).

Editor

If a book has been composed by several authors i.e. consists of various articles, it will normally have been edited by one or two persons who are called "editors". It is easy to recognize whether a person is the author or the editor/compiler since it is indicated by the following notations: "editor(s):", "edited by" or "compiled by". The editor/compiler is treated in the same way as the author but "(Ed.)" or "(Comp.)" should be added in brackets (see also Fig. 8).

Fig. 7: Cataloguing example: title as main entry ▶

NUTRITION FOR DEVELOPING COUNTRIES

WITH SPECIAL REFERENCE TO THE MAIZE CASSAVA AND MILLET AREAS OF AFRICA

MAURICE H. KING
M.D. CANTAB., F.R.C.P. LOND.
WHO Staff Member, the Lembaga Kesehatan Nasional, Surabaya, Indonesia
Formerly Professor of Social Medicine
in the University of Zambia

FELICITY M. A. KING
B.M. OXON., M.R.C.P. LOND.
Formerly Nuffield Research Fellow in Community Paediatrics
in the University of Zambia

DAVID C. MORLEY
M.D. CANTAB., M.R.C.P., D.C.H. LOND.
Reader in Tropical Child Health
in the University of London

H. J. LESLIE BURGESS
M.B.CH.B. ST.AND., D.P.H. LOND., D.T.M. & H. LIVERPOOL, M.P.H. HARVARD
Formerly WHO Area Nutrition Adviser, Malawi

ANN P. BURGESS
B.SC. NUTRITION
Queen Elizabeth College, London

Nairobi Oxford
OXFORD UNIVERSITY PRESS
Dar es Salaam
1972

Title as main entry

NUTRITION   FOR DEVELOPING COUNTRIES

with special reference to the maize,
cassava and millet areas of Africa.
By Maurice H. King et al.
Nairobi et al: Oxford Univ. Press 1972.
no paging, ill.

```
        ← 1st editor

KRISHNA PRASAD, K  (Ed.)

Wood heat for cooking. Edited by ... and
P. Verhaart.  ← 2nd editor
Bangalore: Indian Academy of Sciences
1983. 255 p, fig.
                           acc.-no
```

Fig. 8: Cataloguing example: first and second editors

3.1.2 Corporate Author

If a work has been composed by an institution without mention of a
personal author the institution is called the corporate author. A corporate
author is treated in the same way as a personal author (see Fig. 9).
Quite often institutions are better known under their acronym than under
their full name. (An acronym is a pronounceable abbreviation, a "word",

Fig. 9: Cataloguing example: corporate author

```
       ← corporate author

INSTITUTE OF CULTURAL AFFAIRS INTERNATIONAL
                                    (Ed.)

Directory of rural development projects.
Project descriptions prepared for the
International Exposition of Rural Develop-
ment.
München et al: Saur 1985. 516 p
```

```
┌────────────────────────────────────────────────────┐
│                                                      │
│                                                      │
│     SOCIALLY APPROPRIATE TECHNOLOGY INTER-           │
│        NATIONAL INFORMATION SERVICES                 │
│                                                      │
│                                                      │
│     see:   SATIS                                     │
│                                                      │
│                                                      │
│                                                      │
└────────────────────────────────────────────────────┘
```

Fig. 10: Cataloguing example: "see reference" card

formed by combining initial letters or syllables of a series of words or a compound term.) In that case it will be sufficient to indicate the acronym only. This applies among others to UNIDO, FAO, SATIS, ITDG, and ADB. But as there are always some users who do not know the full name and/or the acronym it is advisable to prepare a **cross-reference card** (Fig. 10) to inform the user under which heading the institutions will be found in the card catalogue. (For cross-reference see also Chapter 3.9, for proceedings see Chapter 3.7.)

But, of course, you have to decide yourself when it will be sufficient to use the acronym. It depends on how well known an institution's acronym is in your country. WALHI in Indonesia, for instance, and CAP in Malaysia are better known under their acronyms than under their full names (Wahana Lingkungan Hidup Indonesia — Indonesian Environmental Forum — and Consumers Association of Penang respectively).

If a **national institution or a government service** is the author, the name of the originating country should be added, even if it is not mentioned on the title page.

Example: PHILIPPINES. MINISTRY OF LABOUR
              TANZANIA. MINISTRY OF LABOUR

This is necessary as there are Ministries of Labour in many countries.

Exception 1: Books and documents published by government institutions of your own country. In such a case it is sufficient to mention the name of the ministry or institution only without prefixing it with the name of your country. But a publication originating from a provincial government of your country should be entered under the province's name, for instance in Malaysia:

SARAWAK. PLANNING UNIT

Exception 2: If the country's name is part of the institution's name such as "Central Bank of India" or "Kenya Industrial Estates" you do not have to repeat/prefix the country's name.

Universities: Works published by universities or their institutes should be entered under the name of the university. The main heading will be the university, followed by the name of the faculty and/or institute.

Example: UNIVERSITAS INDONESIA. FACULTY OF ECO-
NOMICS. INSTITUTE FOR SOCIAL PLANNING

or: UNIVERSITY OF THE PHILIPPINES. COLLEGE OF
AGRICULTURE

3.2 Title

The title is the second item of the entry. In the case of an anonymous work and if there are more than three authors it is the first item of the entry. The title and subtitle, if any, are transcribed in full. The subtitle often explains in detail the content of a publication and/or provides additional information, for instance, that the book covers the proceedings of a conference or seminar. Therefore, it should be fully transcribed if possible. If the subtitle is very long, it may be abridged but in such a way that its meaning will not be changed. Please remember that the title printed on the book cover may sometimes differ from the one printed on

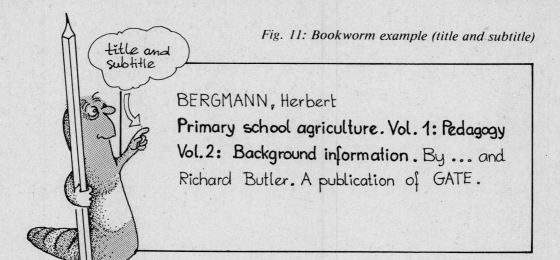

the title page. For cataloguing, the title mentioned on the title page is regarded as the original, as the title proper. The title also includes an indication of the edition, number of volumes and translation (e.g. translated from Malay).

According to international standards **translations** must be indicated including reference to the original language from which the book has been translated. It is not necessary to comply with that rule all the time but it will be helpful to follow it for those books which have been translated into/from your national language and/or a local language respectively and which are available in your library.

Example: David Werner's book "Where there is no doctor" has been translated into many languages. If your library has the English as well as another foreign language version, you should make a note on the English version entry card: (also available in "..." (here follows the respective language) under the title "...") and on the entry card of the local language version you add (also available in English under the title "Where there is no doctor").

Volume

If a publication consists of several volumes, it should be noted on the entry card since this is an important piece of information for the user (see Figs. 12a + b).

FAO AGRICULTURAL SERVICES BULLETIN 12 Suppl. 1

elements
of
agricultural machinery
volume 1

by

robert h. wilkinson

and

oscar a. braunbeck
michigan state university, u.s.a.

agricultural engineering service
agricultural services division

241 pp, 197 fig

FOOD AND AGRICULTURE ORGANIZATION OF THE UNITED NATIONS
Rome 1977

FAO AGRICULTURAL SERVICES BULLETIN 12 Suppl. 2

elements
of
agricultural machinery
volume 2

by

robert h. wilkinson

and

oscar a. braunbeck
michigan state university, u.s.a.

agricultural engineering service
agricultural services division

295 pp, 273 fig

FOOD AND AGRICULTURE ORGANIZATION OF THE UNITED NATIONS
Rome 1977

Fig. 12a: Title page (cataloguing example fig. 12b)

```
    WILKINSON, Robert H

    Elements of agricultural machinery.
    Vol. 1-2. By ... and Oscar A. Braunbeck.
    Rome: FAO 1977. 241,295 p,  197,273 fig.

                                      acc.-no.
    (FAO Agricultural Services Bulletin. No.12,
     Suppl. 1 + 2.)

        number
          of
        volumes
```

Fig. 12b: Cataloguing several volumes

If each volume has a different subtitle, this should also be indicated following the note of how many volumes the publication consists (see Fig. 13).

If there is only one volume available in the library although the complete publication consists of several volumes you should mention it on the entry card (see Fig. 14).

Fig. 13: Cataloguing several volumes with different titles

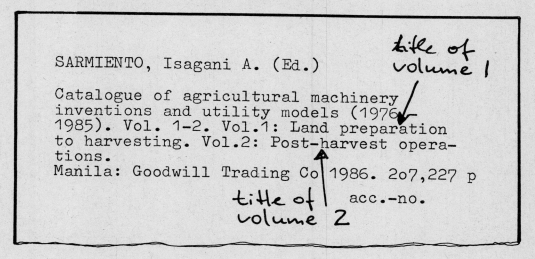

```
    SARMIENTO, Isagani A. (Ed.)          title of
                                         volume 1
    Catalogue of agricultural machinery
    inventions and utility models (1976-
    1985). Vol. 1-2. Vol.1: Land preparation
    to harvesting. Vol.2: Post-harvest opera-
    tions.
    Manila: Goodwill Trading Co 1986. 2o7,227 p

                      title of    acc.-no.
                      volume 2
```

```
BÄNZIGER, H. P.

Hand/foot pumps for village water supply
in developing countries. Part II: Des-
cription of pumps. (Part I is missing)
St. Gallen: SKAT 1982. 1oo p, ill.
```

Fig. 14: Cataloguing several volumes (one missing)

3.3 Imprint

Place of publication, publisher's name, and date of publication make up
the imprint. This information is usually found at the foot and/or on the
back of the title page. It should be indicated on the catalogue card in the
following order: place: publisher's name, date. (Note for typing: the place
is separated from the name by a colon.)

Fig. 15: Bookworm example (imprint)

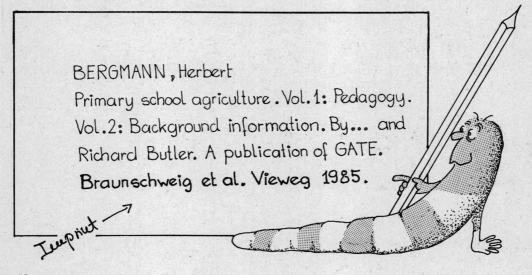

BERGMANN, Herbert
Primary school agriculture. Vol. 1: Pedagogy.
Vol. 2: Background information. By... and
Richard Butler. A publication of GATE.
Braunschweig et al. Vieweg 1985.

Imprint →

Place of publication

Only the town — not the country — has to be mentioned. (But if you feel you should also mention the country in order to provide your users with more detailed information you may of course do so.) If several towns are noted, it is sufficient to indicate the first one only on the catalogue card. Although the title page reads: "Oxford, London, New York ... Oxford University Press", it is sufficient to mention one place/town only:

Oxford et al.: Oxford University Press 1985.

If no place has been given, simply add in brackets "(place unknown)".

Publisher

The publisher's name follows the place of publication. The publisher's name is given in the briefest form in which it can be understood and identified.

If the publisher is identical with the editing institution (= author) it should be given in acronym form if possible provided the majority of your clients are familiar with the acronym. If no mention is made of the publisher you may either use the printer's name (if mentioned) or simply write in brackets "(publisher unknown)".

Date of publication

Following the publisher's name, the date of publication is given in Arabic numerals. In the case of project papers and reports, the respective month of publication should be indicated, as sometimes revised editions of the same paper will be published only months later under the same title but without bearing a note that it is a revised edition. This is especially important for reports of your own organization.

If no date is given in the publication, try to estimate the approximate date on the basis of its content (introduction, foreword, bibliography, tables, etc.). In such a case the date you estimated or found out should be typed in brackets and a question mark should be added: "(1986?)"

Sometimes you may come across several different dates mentioned on the title page and/or the back of the title page. Those dates are either the copyright date (i.e. the year of the first edition), the year(s) of the second or following edition(s), and/or the year(s) of the reprints. In such a case the most recent date should be mentioned on the catalogue card.

3.4 Collation

The physical description of a book is called the collation. It consists of the number of pages, presence of illustrations (maps, graphs, figures, charts, tables), bibliography, and appendices. The collation is indicated on the catalogue card following the date of publication. Please observe punctuation!

    Place: Publisher date. 290 p., ill.   or:

    Place: Publisher date. 114 p., tables, map, bibliogr.

If the publisher did not paginate the book consecutively — this is sometimes the case with conference papers where each article is paginated separately — you should either note "no paging" or "separate paging".

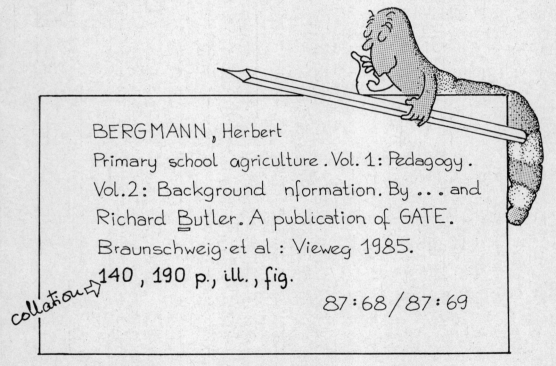

BERGMANN, Herbert

Primary school agriculture. Vol. 1: Pedagogy.

Vol. 2: Background nformation. By ... and

Richard Butler. A publication of GATE.

Braunschweig·et al : Vieweg 1985.

collation⇨ 140 , 190 p., ill. , fig.

87 : 68 / 87 : 69

Fig. 16: Bookworm example (collation)

3.5 Series

A series is defined as a number of separate works/monographs issued in succession by the same publisher and in uniform style with a collective title which generally appears at the head of the title page or on the cover page. The series should be indicated on the catalogue card as it might be an important piece of information for the user. The added entry card for the series will be filed in the title catalogue. **For a small library it will be sufficient to take into account only those series which are of interest to your organization and which have been numbered.** For instance: (FAO Agricultural Services Bulletin. 12. Suppl. 2) or (World Bank Technical Paper. No. 18. Appropriate Technology for Water Supply and Sanitation. Vol. 14). In this case the publication is part of two series (see also Fig. 17).

The series should be indicated at the end of the entry and in brackets. Do not forget to note the series number if one is given by the publisher.

```
URBAN SANITATION PLANNING MANUAL

based on the Jakarta case study. By
Vincent Zajac et al.
Washington: World Bank 1984. 158 p,
drawings
                                acc.-no.

(World Bank Technical Paper No.18.
Appropriate Technology for Water Supply
and Sanitation. Vol. 14.)
```
series ↗

Fig. 17: Cataloguing example: series

3.6 Cataloguing Serials (Excluding Periodicals)

A publication issued at regular intervals, i.e. every 1−2 years, and containing new or updated data and new figures basically the same subject is a serial.

The publication of a serial is intended to continue indefinitely. More often than not its author/editor is a corporate one i.e. a national or international institution. The title will probably remain the same over the years and often reads like "(Statistical) Yearbook ...", "Annual Report ...", "Economic Survey ..." or "Agricultural/Population/Foreign Trade Statistics", or "Almanac". But even if these terms are not used in the title or subtitle, serials can easily be distinguished from 'normal' monographs as the year(s) beinh reported is/are usually mentioned on the title page.

Cataloguing these books is quite simple, as there will be only one main entry card for the first one available in the library. All following editions will merely be added (see Fig. 18). When new yearbooks, annual reports, etc., arrive in the library it is necessary to first check whether one or several previous editions are already in the library. In this case you only have to add the new data, i.e. year(s) which the book records, year of publication, number of pages, and accession number.

In the example given below (Fig. 18) the first year mentioned is the year under review, the next one stands for the year of publication. Then the collation and the accession number follow.

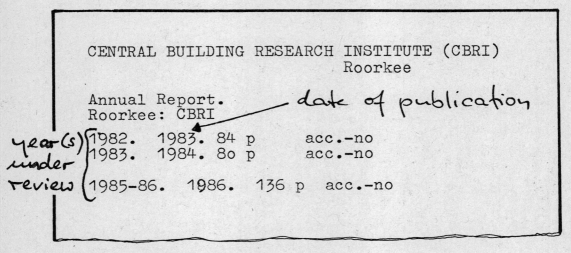

Fig. 18: Cataloguing example: serial

In exceptional cases a publication may be a serial as well as a series. In such a case you may disregard the series, i.e. you do not have to indicate the series notation on the catalogue card.

Example: The FAO Production Yearbooks are part of the numbered FAO Statistics Series. The fact that these yearbooks are part of a serial is more important than the fact that they are part of a series. Therefore, the respective catalogue card will read:

46

```
FOOD AND AGRICULTURE ORGANIZATION (FAO)

FAO production yearbook. English - French -
Spanish. Vol.
Rome: FAO

Vol. 36. 1982.  1983.  32o p   acc.-no
Vol. 37. 1983.  1984.  32o p   acc.-no
Vol. 38.  missing
Vol. 39. 1985.  1986.  372 p   acc.-no
Vol. 4o. 1986.  1987.  3o6 p   acc.-no
```

*Fig. 19: Cataloguing example: series and serial at the same time. (Series notation has
been disregarded)*

3.7 Proceedings

Proceedings of international and national conferences, seminars, or
workshops are often published in book form. These publications should
be treated in the same way as any other book. There is no reason to treat
them differently and place them separately on the shelves as some libraries
do. Generally, there is an editor, a title and subtitle, an imprint and a

Fig. 20: Cataloguing proceedings (corporate editor)

```
RESEARCH CENTER FOR APPLIED SCIENCE AND
    TECHNOLOGY (RECAST), Tribhuvan Univ.

Renewable energy resources in Nepal. Pro-
ceedings of the workshop seminar Kathmandu,
1-4 April 1981. Sponsored by ... and orga-
nized by RECAST in collaboration with Swiss
Federal Institute of Technology et al.
Kathmandu: Sahayogi Press 1981. 277 p, ill.,
tables
                              acc.-no
```

```
NESTEL, Barry (Ed.)

Agricultural research for development:
Potentials and challenges in Asia. Report
of a conference, Jakarta, Indonesia, Oct.
24-29, 1982. Sponsored by German Foundation
for International Development (DSE). Organized
by International Federation of Agricultural
Research Systems for Development (IFARD) and
International Service for National Agricul-
tural Research (ISNAR).
The Hague: ISNAR 1983. 6o p       acc.-no
```

Fig. 21: Cataloguing proceedings (personal editor)

collation — so why not catalogue and store the publication in the same way as any other publication in your library? In Fig. 20 + 21 you will find two examples of how to catalogue proceedings.

3.8 Added Entries

An added entry serves to refer the user to secondary entries such as second and/or third author, title, series, and additional class numbers. A duplication of the main entry card is used as an added entry card. Large libraries such as the Library of Congress and national libraries all over the world usually indicate the added entries on the main entry card by adding at the bottom of the card notations (the technical term for such notations is "tracing") such as I. Title, II. Joint author or editor, III. Editing institution, IV. Series. Since the information needed for the added entries is already indicated in the main entry, we do not think it necessary to repeat the secondary entries. It is sufficient to mark the added entry by underlining the first letter of the respective secondary entry (see Figs. 22 and 23). Although international rules do not require an added entry for the publishing/editing institution, nevertheless it is recommended in some cases. Users often remember the publishing/editing institution and not the respective personal author. The user will ask, for example, for a book

← Main entry

URBAN SANITATION PLANNING MANUAL

based on the Jakarta case study. By
Vincent Zajac et al.
Washington: World Bank 1984. 158 p,
drawings ← 2nd added entry: editing institution

(World Bank Technical Paper. No 18.
Appropriate Technology for Water Supply
and Sanitation. Vol. 14.)

1st added entry: author

↑ 3rd added entry: series

Fig. 22: Marking added entries

Fig. 23: Bookworm example (added entries)

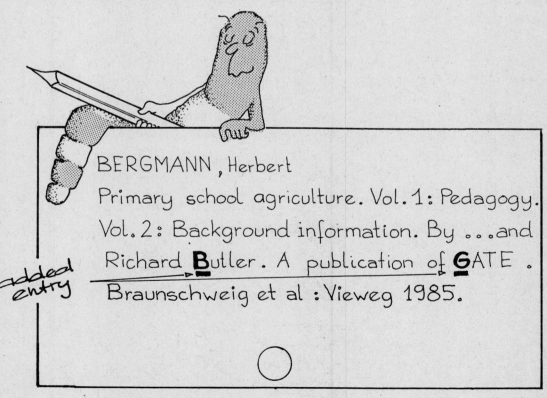

BERGMANN, Herbert
Primary school agriculture. Vol. 1: Pedagogy.
Vol. 2: Background information. By ...and
Richard Butler. A publication of GATE.
Braunschweig et al : Vieweg 1985.

added entry

```
ITDG


see also:   Intermediate Technology
            Publications   or IT Publ.
```

Fig. 24: "see also" reference card

published by ITDG on construction. You refer him to the author catalogue but he cannot find it there; then you refer him to the classified catalogue, to the subgroup "construction" but again he cannot find it. He
will then be convinced that the book he is looking for is not available in
the library. Some time later, just by chance, you discover that the book is
in your library but that it has been entered under the personal author's
name of Harald K. Dancy and that ITGD is the publisher only. In order to
be able to answer this kind of enquiry it is advisable to prepare added
entries for the publishing institution, e.g. ITDG and Intermediate Technology Publications respectively. But please do not forget to type "see
also" references (see Figs. 24 and 25 and Chapter 3.9).
The same applies to GATE publications: there is always a personal or
corporate author and for this reason the main entry will always be made
under that author. But unlike ITDG which has its own publishing compa-

Fig. 25: "see also" reference card

```
INTERMEDIATE TECHNOLOGY PUBLICATIONS /
        IT PUBLICATIONS



see also:  ITDG
```

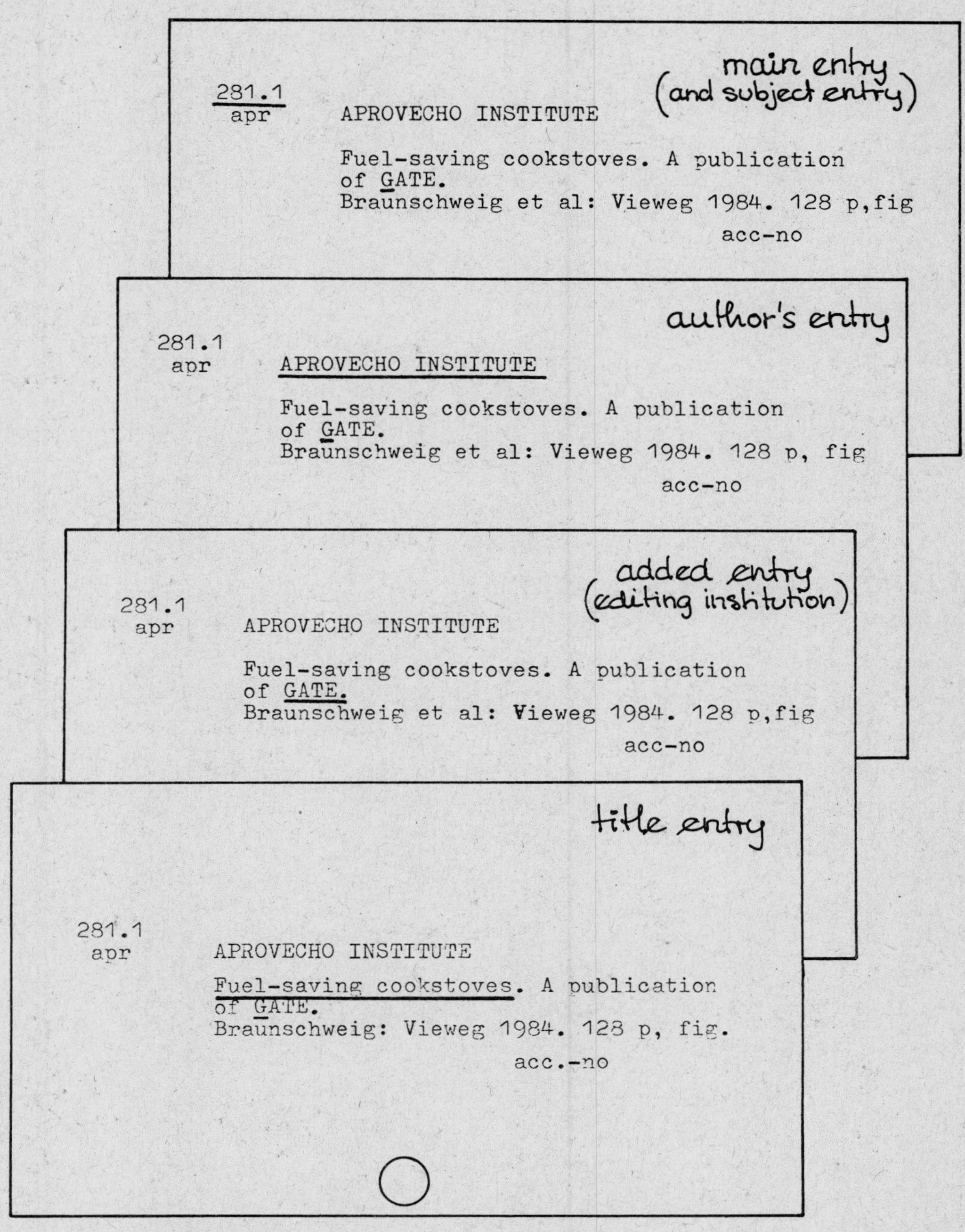

Fig. 26: Underlining added entries

ny — Intermediate Technology Publications — GATE has most of its books published through the commercial publisher Vieweg. On the title page you will always find the note "A publication of Deutsches Zentrum für Entwicklungstechnologien — GATE in: Deutsche Gesellschaft für Technische Zusammenarbeit (GTZ) GmbH". But you only have to write "A publication of GATE" and use GATE in this subtitle for the added entry (see Fig. 26).

3.9 Cross-References

Cross-reference cards refer users from terms or names not used to those which are in the catalogue. This kind of cross reference is called **'see'** **reference.** If, for instance, you decide to use the acronym 'VITA' instead of 'Volunteers in Technical Assistance', you should prepare the following card and enter it in the author catalogue:

```
    VOLUNTEERS   IN   TECHNICAL   ASSISTANCE


    see:   VITA
```

Fig. 27: "see" reference card

If two different expressions/terms/names are used equally in the catalogues for the same corporate author for instance, it is necessary to refer the user to both terms. Such references are called **"see also" references.** They may be used for organizations which changed their names or which are known under two different names.

Example 1: Change of name of a country

Ceylon, for instance, changed its name in 1972 to Sri Lanka. All official government publications before 1972 are published under "Ceylon, ...".

Fig. 28: "see also" reference card

In order not to have to change all catalogue cards with Ceylon, a 'see also' reference card is sufficient; it will refer the user to both entries.

Example 2: Change of name of an institution

Sometimes institutions change their names — for example, ministries under a new government. In such a case a 'see also' reference is needed.

```
CENTRAL PLANNING ORGANIZATION
                        (old name)


see also:   MINISTRY OF PLANNING
                        (new name)
```

Fig. 29: "see also reference" card

```
MINISTRY OF PLANNING
                (new name)



see also: CENTRAL PLANNING ORGANIZATION
                        (old name)
```

Example 3: Institutions known under two names

The main entry of a document is made under "International Bank for Reconstruction and Development (IBRD)" as written on the title page. There may be some users who only remember that the document they are looking for has been published by the World Bank. The IBRD is part of the World Bank and some users might not know that. In order to guarantee that all documents of an institution/organization which a user is looking for will be retrieved it is advisable to prepare a 'see also' reference card. In the above-mentioned case you should write: "World Bank see also: International Bank for Reconstruction and Development (IBRD)" and "International Bank for Reconstruction and Development (IBRD) see also: World Bank".

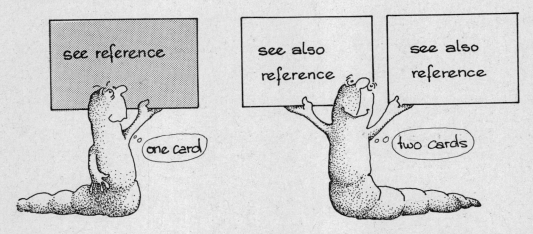

Remember: For a 'see' reference one reference card is needed and for a 'see also' reference two reference cards.

3.10 Form of the Catalogue Card

As we have already emphasized, uniformity is important in library organization. Uniformity is also necessary regarding the form of the catalogue card, i.e. the way you arrange and type the information describing the elements of a book on the catalogue card.
If certain standards and a generally accepted order are maintained throughout your work, users will easily recognize the elements they are

54

looking for. They will know, for instance, that the title will usually follow the author and that the collation will follow the imprint.

A generally accepted order is outlined below (see also Fig. 30):

1. **Author** (or title for anonymous works)
2. **Title**
   —Subtitle
   —Second and third authors — if any — or any other information regarding the author/editor (e.g. editing institution)
   —Number of volumes (also the individual subtitles if given)
   —Edition (if 2nd or following), reprint
3. **Imprint**
   —Place of publication (or of printer if publisher is unknown)
   —Name of publisher (or printer)
   —Date of publication
4. **Collation**
   —Number of pages
   —Illustrations
5. **Series and number of series**
6. **Accession number**

The bibliographic elements have been described and now we will describe the content and proceed to classifying or indexing.

```
14.08
sto
            STOLL, Gaby

            Natural crop protection based on
            local farm resources in the Tropics
            and Subtropics. (Editing institution:
            AGRECOL).
            Gaimersheim: Margraf 1986. 186 p
                                       87:123


            (series, if any)
```

Fig. 30: Sample catalogue card (original size 14.8 × 10.5 cm)

Fig. 31: Bookworm example (bibliographic description completed)

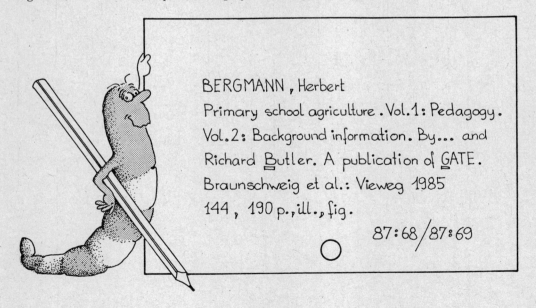

```
BERGMANN , Herbert
Primary school agriculture . Vol.1: Pedagogy.
Vol.2: Background information. By... and
Richard Butler. A publication of GATE.
Braunschweig et al.: Vieweg 1985
144 , 190 p.,ill.,fig.
                            87:68/87:69
```

4. Classification

4.1 Why is a Classification Scheme Needed?

A library classification is a pre-established scheme which groups concepts/subjects into classes and which uses mostly hierarchical relations for the arrangement of classes: main classes with divisions and subdivisions.

In classification schemes the concepts/subjects are preceded with their code number, also called classification or class number. In the following we are going to use the term "class number".

A classification scheme provides subject access to the books and at the same time serves to determine the proper location of a publication on the shelves.

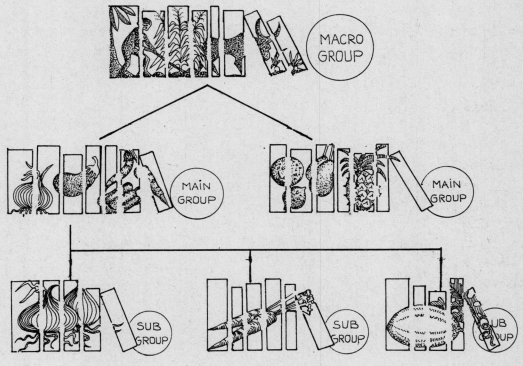

Libraries and documentation centres which arrange their collection in an open-shelf system particularly need a classification scheme in order to shelve books together with other publications on the same subject and near to publications on related subjects. Most libraries throughout the world use an open-shelf arrangement. For the library user, it is extremely helpful to find all publications related to the subject he is looking for in the same location.

In Chapter 6 "Indexing" we will discuss the assignment of subject headings or indexing which also provides subject access to the library collection. The only difference between classifying and indexing is the tool used for the content description. In classification schemes, the subject headings are preceded with their code number and arranged systematically. In lists of subject headings and thesauri, the subject headings or descriptors are arranged in alphabetical order.

However, indexing or contents description with subject headings does not serve to determine the actual place of a book on the shelves.

In classifying, the main class number which corresponds to the main subject of a publication serves at the same time as the call number.

A **call number** is assigned to a book to distinguish it from others and to indicate its place on the shelves. A call number is usually composed of two elements: the main class number and the first three letters of the main heading (author's name or title for anonymous works). See also Chapter 11.2.

Before the procedure of classifying documents is described in Chapter 5, we would like first to present various classification systems.

4.2 Various Classification Systems

There are basically two types of classification systems, i.e.
—the universal classification systems and
—the special classification systems.
The universal classification systems cover the whole of human knowledge as represented in books and arrange it in broad subject classes (also called groups). Special classification systems do not claim to cover all knowledge but only the related fields of knowledge in which they specialize. The most widely used universal classification systems in English-speaking countries are
—DEWEY DECIMAL CLASSIFICATION (DDC)
—UNIVERSAL DECIMAL CLASSIFICATION (UDC)
—LIBRARY OF CONGRESS CLASSIFICATION (LC).
Although these classification systems are rather complicated and very detailed, they are quite popular in the United States as small libraries can purchase processed catalogue cards which also include the class number (DDC or LC). For small documentation centres in Third World countries where such a service is not available and where the librarian has to do the classifying, these systems are not recommended.
Nevertheless the DDC, which is the most widespread one, shall be briefly outlined in order to demonstrate the structure of universal classification systems. UDC and DDC are very similar in their structure.

4.3 DEWEY DECIMAL CLASSIFICATION (DDC)

In the Dewey Decimal Classification all knowledge is divided into ten classes. Each class number is subdivided by 10, these again by 10, and then each number by decimals. The structure allows the library to classify as broadly or as specifically as its collection and purpose demand. For smaller libraries the abridged version is sufficient.

The ten classes of DDC are as follows:

000   General Works
100   Philosophy
200   Religion
300   Social Sciences
400   Language
500   Pure Science
600   Technology
700   The Arts
800   Literature
900   History

To illustrate the system we will trace two subjects — pottery and sorghum — through their steps but omit the intervening numbers:

600   Technology
  660   Chemical and Related Technologies
    666   Ceramic and Allied Technologies
      666.3   Pottery
      666.4   Pottery Processes and Equipment
and:

600   Technology
  630   Agriculture and Related Technologies
    633   Field Crops
      633.1   Cereal Grain
        633.17   Millet and Related Crops
          633.174   Grain Sorghums

As you can see from these examples, the three-digit classes are sufficient for small libraries; in some cases, it may be necessary to use the four-digit classes. If a library has, for instance, only ten or twenty books in its entire language group, all these books could be placed with the general language group 400 and no subdivisions are needed.

4.4 The SATIS Classification System

There is a great variety of special classification systems but only one in the field of appropriate technology, i.e. the SATIS classification system.
The SATIS classification system was developed in the late seventies by several European AT-organizations. The first edition was published in 1979, the second revised edition, which is still current, in 1983. The SATIS classification system is used by many AT NGOs throughout the world.
SATIS divides the knowledge related to AT into eight main subject groups called 'macro-groups':

1. **Man and Society**
2. **Energy and Power**
3. **Water, Sanitation and Waste Disposal**
4. **Agriculture, Forestry Works, and Aquaculture and Fisheries**
5. **Agricultural Products Processing and Food Production**
6. **Manufacture, Engineering and Services**
7. **Building and Construction Works**
8. **Health**

Again we will illustrate the system by tracing the subjects pottery and sorghum through their steps:

6.   Manufacture, Engineering and Services
  660   Manufacture of Non-Metallic Mineral Products
    661   Pottery and Ceramics
      — clay products, china and earthenware, pottery kilns
and:

4.   Agriculture ...
  440   Cultivation of Crops
    441   Amylaceous Crops
      441.1   Cereals
        441.14   Sorghum

As you can see from these examples, the SATIS system is also quite complicated and some macro-groups — particularly group ''4-Agriculture''

— have been subdivided in such a detailed way that it may be confusing for some small libraries. It can be assumed that SATIS designed its classification scheme primarily for comparatively large documentation centres specializing in energy, agriculture, or water and sanitation. For documentation centres specializing in these fields, the classification system allows very detailed indexing.

But small libraries do not need to index their documents in a very detailed way, and therefore do not need a very detailed classification system. If, for instance, you do not have more than five documents on wind energy in your library, it is not only unnecessary but also confusing to place each of them with different classes. Though some people believe that classifying becomes easier the more subject classes there are, the opposite is true.

If you take into consideration that the majority of AT documentation centres do not have more than 5000 volumes (the average is about 2000 volumes) and that the SATIS classification has approximately 720 groups/classes, it becomes clear that it is too extensive. That would mean there would be only three to seven books in each group which would be confusing for both the librarian and the user. For a small library, approximately 200 classes/groups should be sufficient.

Those of you who are already using the SATIS system can of course go on using it. But it is advisable to use the three-digit groups only, and to adapt the classification to your own purposes and needs. GATE, for instance, modified the SATIS classification according to its needs and other AT NGOs have done the same.

Despite the inconsistencies and drawbacks of the SATIS classification system (nobody is perfect!), we do recommend its use for AT NGOs with large collections as there is no other one specifically designed for AT organizations. For those who are using the SATIS classification system we will also give the respective SATIS class numbers while explaining how to classify in Chapter 5.

4.5 RURAL DEVELOPMENT CLASSIFICATION (RDC) — Model

For small libraries not specializing in one or two subjects only, the author has developed a classification model (see Annex I). By using the term "model", special emphasis is put on the fact that the classification system can/should be used for and adapted to specific needs; it may be abridged or expanded, or used the way it has been presented.

The Rural Development Classification (RDC) Model is primarily intended to serve the needs of those NGOs which are working in the wide field of rural development and appropriate technology. Ideally, it should meet the needs of very small libraries (around 500 to 1000 titles) as well as of larger ones (up to 10,000 titles). In order to meet these requirements the classification scheme has been laid out in three levels:

Level 1 consists of 21 macro-groups.

Level 2 consists of the 21 macro-groups and about 170 main groups, i.e. subdivisions of the macro-groups.

Level 3 consists of the 21 macro-groups, the 170 main groups and approximately 50 sub groups. Only those main groups have been subdivided of which a subdivision could be expected to be of interest to the majority of users. According to your specific needs further subdivisions are, of course, possible.

For all three levels an alphabetical index of terms/descriptors has been prepared in order to make the classifying job easier. The index not only lists all those terms used in the classification scheme but also includes descriptors which are thought to be important though not important enough to be included in the classification scheme itself.

There are several ways to implement this classification system:

1. Only the 21 macro-groups (= level 1, always ending with .00) are used. Such a practice is recommended only for libraries with a very small collection (approx. 500 titles) which is not expected to grow much.

2. The main groups, level 2 (4 digit groups, i.e. 10.03 = AT), are used as a basis. If you think this level is still too detailed for your needs, you may, of course, delete those main groups that are not relevant.
3. The complete classification system is used (macro-, main and sub-groups).

With the exception of those small libraries which are only using the 21 macro-groups, the macro-groups (always ending with .00) should not be used for classifying, asthey are more of a heading than a class/group. If you want to assign a more or less general class number you should use the ones ending with '.01'.

4.5.1 Possible Expansion of the RDC

In case you need further subdivisions the ones already proposed may be used and additional subdivisions can be set up by either following the SATIS classification or installing your own subdivisions. If, for instance, you need subdivisions for "15.02-Plant Protection" you can easily establish them by using either all or only some of the subdivisions established by SATIS for "Plant Protection: 433", i.e. the ones which you regard as necessary. Example:

15.02   Plant Protection
   15.02.01   Plant Diseases and Control
   15.02.02   Pest Control

The same principle may be applied to other main groups. For some organizations it might, for instance, be necessary to subdivide "15.04 — Cereals" into

15.04.01   Rice
15.04.02   Maize/Corn
15.04.03   Wheat
15.04.04   Sorghum
15.04.05   Millet
15.04.06   Others

Still other organizations might only need the subdivisions for rice and maize/corn.

For other organizations it might be important to install geographical sub-divisions. If you intend to collect documents especially on your country/region it is helpful to set up such subdivisions, for example:

02.04   Regional Development and Planning
   02.04.01   Rural Development
   02.04.02   Rural Development in ... (here follows the name of your country/region/province)

or another example:

08.04   Pollution
   08.04.01   Air Pollution
   08.04.02   Water Pollution
   08.04.03   Soil Pollution
   08.04.04   Pollution in ... (name of the country).

Such subdivisions may be added to all those groups which are of major importance to your organization and under which you already have a considerable number of documents.

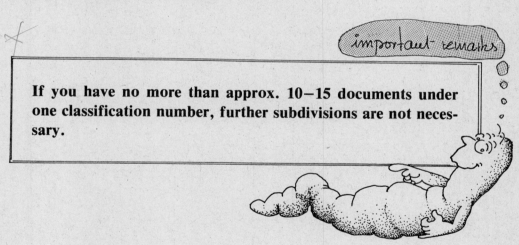

important remarks

If you have no more than approx. 10—15 documents under one classification number, further subdivisions are not necessary.

You may also use only those subdivisions which are relevant to your needs. The complete version of the RDC suggests subdivisions for some main groups but you might not need all of them.

Example: For the main group ''06.11 — Religion'' the following sub-groups (in alphabetical order) are proposed:

06.11.01   Buddhism
06.11.02   Christianity
06.11.03   Hinduism
06.11.04   Islam
06.11.05   Others

NGOs in Africa will most probably not have documents on Buddhism and Hinduism. If they do need subdivisions at all, they could subdivide as follows:

06.11.01   Christianity
06.11.02   Islam
06.11.03   Others

For some NGOs in Latin America the subgroup "Christianity" only might possibly be of relevance, and therefore it is sufficient to only establish one subdivision: 06.11.01 Christianity. Others might still need further subdivision(s), i.e. "Liberation Theology" and/or "Church and Development; Church and Society", thus creating the following subdivisions:

06.11.01   Christianity
06.11.02   Liberation Theology incl. Church and Development

So you see there are many possibilities to adapt the classification to your needs but even the best classification system is just a tool for classifying and does not do the job itself. So let's go on to the most important but also most difficult step in information processing: classifying!

5. Classifying

In Chapter 3 we said that cataloguing is the bibliographic description of a document. On the basis of that definition we can now say: **Classifying is the contents description of a document by which the main subject and possibly one or two secondary subjects are determined.**
The problem of how to determine or choose the right subjects and thus the right class numbers will be discussed below. This step in information processing is called classifying. Before describing the general principles of classifying, it should be pointed out that there are two possible uses of a classification system.

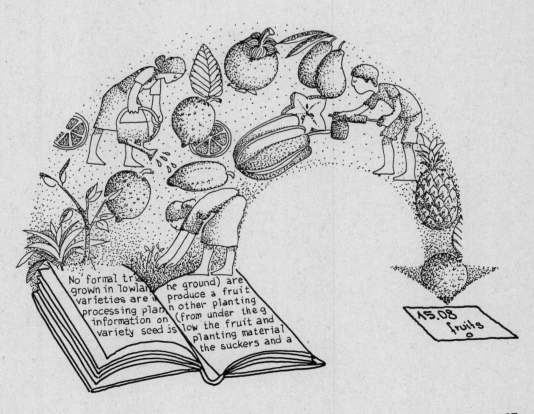

a) **The classification system primarily serves the DETERMINATION OF THE CALL NUMBER,** i.e. of the actual place a document will have on the shelf. In such a case, one class number only will be assigned to each book. For a more detailed description of the content, subject headings, also called descriptors, are assigned.

b) **The classification system is used for CONTENTS DESCRIPTION AS WELL AS THE DETERMINATION OF THE CALL NUMBER.** If necessary, several class numbers can be assigned: the main class number which at the same time serves as the call number and additional secondary class numbers for more in-depth description of the content.

The advantage of a classified arrangement of documents on the shelves and of the cards in the card catalogue lies in the fact that it brings together closely related documents in a logical sequence, from the general to the more specific. Thus, the user can look for information by browsing not only from the general to the specific but also from the specific to the general. For open-shelf arrangement a classification is indispensable.

However, the classified arrangement requires the user to have some knowledge of the classification system and of the structure of the discipline. An alphabetical index can help in gaining access to the system. In order to enable any new library users to gain fast and easy access to the library holdings a librarian should provide them with an introduction (in a written or oral form) to the structure of its classification scheme.

Although contents description or indexing is best done by assigning descriptors or subject headings, we do not recommend it for small libraries as it is rather difficult and requires a lot of experience (see also Chapter 6). For the target group of this manual it should be sufficient to do contents description by assigning several class numbers. **But no more than three class numbers should be assigned to one book!** In individual cases exceptions are allowed. If the classification is used in this way no subject headings (except geographical ones) are needed.

In any case it is essential to only assign one such call number or physical location to each title. Even if you have several copies of a book, you should not assign different call numbers to the various copies and subsequently put them in different places! **The call number, the main class number, should always be the same for documents consisting of several volumes or of which you have several copies.**

Classifying is the most important and most time-consuming task in the library. So please do not get nervous if it takes you an hour or more to decide on the right class number. If you think a specific book is too difficult to classify correctly, put it aside and try again the next day. It might also be helpful to ask colleagues for their opinion regarding the best class number when dealing with a "difficult" document; do not be afraid to ask them in which class they would expect the document to be placed.

While classifying you should always remember that a book not properly classified will probably be lost to the library unless the author is known. It is nearly impossible to classify a book by just looking at the title and/or subtitle since they are sometimes misleading, i.e. they do not represent the content of the book in a brief form as expected. That is why you should also skim through the table of contents, the preface, and the introduction. It might be even necessary to read parts of the book.

5.1 Principles of Classifying

When classifying the following principles should be observed:[1]

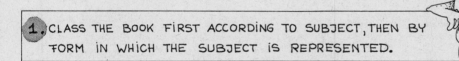

1. CLASS THE BOOK FIRST ACCORDING TO SUBJECT, THEN BY FORM IN WHICH THE SUBJECT IS REPRESENTED.

This is the basic principle of classifying and the easiest to follow as it is obvious that the content is more important than the form. But again the exception proves the rule: in some generalia classes (Dictionaries and Maps and Atlases, for instance) the form is more important and in such cases a book will be classified according to form.

Following the principle of **classifying a book first by subject,** we should classify a book entitled 'History of the AT Movement'[2] with "Appro-

---

[1] The following principles (1–5) closely follow the principles as quoted in: Wynar: Introduction to Cataloging and Classification. 5th ed. pages 253-255.

[2] The examples of titles mentioned on the following pages are fictitious if not stated otherwise.

priate Technology'' (SATIS: 103; RDC: 10.03) and not with ''History'' since appropriate technology is the main subject. A book entitled 'Solar Energy in Buildings' should be classified with ''Building Design specific to Environment'' or ''Solar Architecture'' (SATIS: 712; RDC: 21.04.01) as in this case the aspect of a specific building design is more important to the reader than the one on solar energy.

Classifying according to the form in which the publication is presented is not difficult as long as there specific group ''General Works (or Generalia)''. A dictionary no matter which language or which subject should always be classified with ''Dictionaries'' (RDC: 01.02; at present no class in SATIS). But a bibliography on a specific subject should be placed with that subject as the user might be interested in obtaining information about additional sources. And a map or atlas no matter which region or topic it deals with should always be placed with ''Maps and Atlases'' (RDC: 01.03; at present no class in SATIS).

When we are talking about classifying according to the form we should also mention **fiction** as some NGOs not only have non-fiction but also fiction (novels, stories, children's books). Generally, this kind of book does not figure in the libraries we have been talking about so far but it cannot be neglected.

I suggest you simply put all fiction books on a shelf at the very end of your collection. If necessary you may distinguish between fiction for adults and children's books. You do not have to classify fiction but the books should be catalogued. Their call number consists of one element only, i.e. the first three letters of the author's name.

In order to distinguish fiction from non-fiction you could additionally use a different colour for the call number labels. The catalogue cards — for author and title catalogue — should be filed together with the other ones. In exceptional cases fiction is treated like non-fiction, i.e. such books will be classified. Example: An organization in Papua New Guinea published books on good gardening and the environment in the form of fiction or stories. Such books have not been written in order to entertain people but to educate them. Therefore, they should be placed with the appropriate class, i.e. with gardening and environment respectively.

2. CLASS A BOOK WHERE IT WILL BE MOST USEFUL.

This means that the classifier has to take into consideration the nature of the collection and the needs of the user.

Example: Your library has so far only a few books on organic agriculture although that subject is an important part of your organization's work. While classifying a book entitled 'Agricultural Systems', you find out that two of the book's six chapters deal with organic agriculture, and in such a case you should classify the book with "Organic Farming" (SATIS: 404; RDC: 14.03) and not with a more general class since the book is obviously needed in the specific class.

A book entitled 'Appropriate Technology for Women' which mainly describes various appropriate technologies should not be placed with "Women and Development" but with "Appropriate Technology" (SATIS: 103; RDC: 10.03 or 10.03.01) as the technologies described may be applied by men as well. On the other hand, a book with nearly the same title, let's say 'Women and Appropriate Technology', which mainly deals with the social and economic aspects of the subject, i.e. access of women to technology, should be placed with "Women and Development" (SATIS: 118; RDC: 06.04) and not with "Appropriate Technology". In both cases a second class number may be assigned to the book in order to refer the user to the other aspect.

Here is another example:

A book entitled 'Evaluation of Rural Development Projects' should be classified with "Project Planning and Evaluation" (SATIS: 116; RDC: 02.03) as it describes an evaluation technique which may be applied to other projects as well. The secondary class number will be for "Rural Development" (SATIS: 113; RDC: 02.04.01). But the book 'Evaluation of the Rural Development Project in the Kandy District/Sri Lanka' should be classified with "Rural Development" (SATIS: 113; RDC: 02.04.01 or 02.04.02 if you introduced a geographical subgroup) as it deals with specific problems in rural development and not with theoretical evaluation techniques.

71

From these examples you see that you should always ask yourself: Where will the book serve the user's needs best and where will the user expect to find it?

---

3. CLASS A BOOK ACCORDING TO ITS MOST SPECIFIC SUBJECT RATHER THAN IN THE GENERAL TOPIC.

In this respect it is helpful to study the classification scheme thoroughly, primarily in order to answer such questions as: "What is the specific broader subject embracing the sub-topics?" or: "How is this subject subdivided in the classification schedule?" It is quite obvious that, if you assign a single number to all books on "Water and Sanitation" and fail to subdivide them by specific subjects, the result will be a discouragingly large assortment of volumes under one number and that impairs the effectiveness of the collection. Too many books under one class number make it difficult for the user to find the one he is looking for. For instance, a book entitled 'Schooling in Zimbabwe' should be placed with "Primary Education" (SATIS: 171; RDC: 07.05) as it mainly deals with primary education and not with "Education and Training" in general (SATIS: 170; RDC: 07.01) even if the title sounds quite general. Please remember not to use the macro-groups (ending with .00) for classifying.

---

4. WHEN THE BOOK DEALS WITH TWO OR THREE SUBJECTS, PLACE IT WITH THE PREDOMINANT SUBJECT OR WITH THE ONE TREATED FIRST.

If two subjects are treated equally in a book the book should be placed in the class of the first subject. For example, a book entitled 'Wind-mills and Watermills' should be classified with "Windmills" (SATIS: 246; RDC: 20.12) since windmills is the subject mentioned first. The secondary class numbers should be "Water Wheels/Watermills (SATIS: 252/255; RDC: 20.13).

If a document treats three subjects it will be placed in the class of the subject which is treated most fully.

72

The GATE publication "Technological Development for Village Women in Mali" deals with three subjects: 1. Women and Development, 2. Shea-butter Production/Vegetable Oil Processing, and 3. Dissemination of a New Technology. Since the above publication treats the social aspect, i.e. women and development, most fully, the main class number will be 06.04. Secondary class numbers should be assigned for 'Vegetable Oil Processing': 15.06 and 'Dissemination Strategies': 02.03.

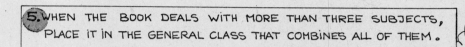

5. WHEN THE BOOK DEALS WITH MORE THAN THREE SUBJECTS, PLACE IT IN THE GENERAL CLASS THAT COMBINES ALL OF THEM.

A book dealing for example to the same extent with the cultivation and processing of rice, cassava, maize, and garden vegetables, should be placed with the 'General Works' group within Plant Production and Processing, i.e. 15.01, and not with any of the subgroups. Additionally, secondary class numbers can be assigned.

> **In order to classify books of similar subjects consistently it is advisable to cross-check the intended class number with the books that have already been assigned that class number to make sure it actually fits into that group. This can be done by either checking the already classified books directly on the shelves or in the classified card catalogue.**

classifying our example:

After having studied the principles of classifying let us now classify together our example whose tables of contents are given in Fig. 1.

First, we will look at the title and the subtitle and identify the following key words:

Primary School
Agriculture
Pedagogy.

When we read the table of contents we can identify additional subjects:

Teaching Methods
Crops
Crop Storage.

Now we have to master the most difficult task and decide which of the above subjects is the main one and therefore which main class number (call number) will be assigned. After having carefully studied the table of contents and the preface and glancing through the two volumes, I come to the conclusion that AGRICULTURE is the main subject. Although one could be tempted to split the work and place volume 1 with "Education and Training" and volume 2 with "Agriculture", please remember that you are not allowed to do so in any circumstances. The call number for the complete publication (both volumes) must be the same. It should be classed in "14.00-Agriculture".

Now we take the RDC classification scheme and study the entire group 14.00 in order to assign the most relevant or specific class number. Since the volumes cover several subjects within "Agriculture" to nearly the same extent (see principle 5), i.e. AGRICULTURAL TRAINING, ORGANIC FARMING/ECO-FARMING, PLANT PROTECTION, and STORAGE, we will assign the broad class number "14.01-Agriculture" as this class also comprises works covering several divisions. Our call number will thus be

$$\boxed{\begin{array}{c} 14.01 \\ \text{ber} \end{array}}$$

But we are not allowed to neglect the subjects PEDAGOGY, PRIMARY SCHOOL and CROPS which are not yet covered by the main class number. We therefore assign the following secondary class numbers:

07.03 Teaching Methods
07.05 Primary Education
15.01 Plant/Crop Production and Processing

Now our example is catalogued and classified and ready for typing. The work slip is now completed and looks like this:

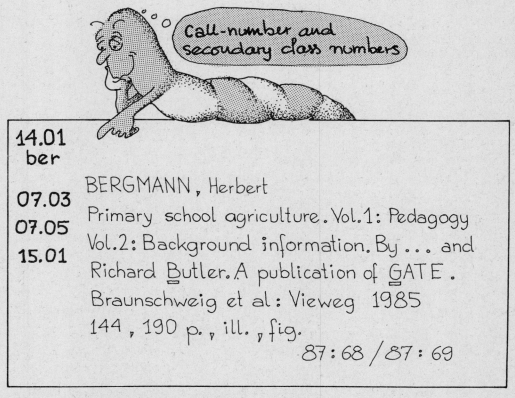

Fig. 32: Bookworm example (classified)

5.2 Step-by-Step Guide to Classifying

Since classifying is the most important task in a library, it must be done well. A step-by-step guide to classifying is given below although some of it is repetition.[1]

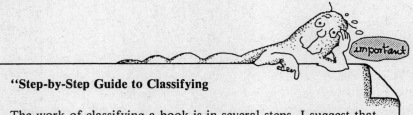

"Step-by-Step Guide to Classifying

The work of classifying a book is in several steps. I suggest that the reader go over the following questions once or twice, then apply the steps to individual books that come up for classifying.

Step 1 Is it a book about something (about a rice thresher, for example, or about fishponds), or is it a book of a certain kind (an atlas, for example, or a dictionary)?

Step 2 If it is a book about something, is the entire book about the same thing or does it deal with several subjects?

Step 3 If it deals with one subject, name that subject. Match that name with the narrowest of the established classes that will fit and assign the corresponding class number to the book.

Step 4 If it deals with several subjects, can these subjects all be said to be sub-topics of one broader topic? If so, name the broader topic and match that name with the best-fitting of the established classes. Assign the corresponding class number(s) to the book.

Step 5 If it deals with several subjects that cannot be said to be sub-topics of one broader topic, name the topic that is either most thoroughly covered or of predominant interest to the type of user for whom the library exists. Match that name with the best-fitting of the established classes. Assign the corresponding class number(s) to the book.

Step 6 If it is not a book about something so much as a book of a certain format, name that format (dictionary? encyclopedia? almanac? collection of tables? bibliography?) and match that name with the best-fitting of the established classes. Assign the corresponding class number(s) to the book."

[1]   Hoffman, Herbert H.: Small library cataloging. Santa Ana, Calif.: Headway Publ. 1977. Pages 32-33. The text has been slightly modified as regards examples and some terms.

6. Indexing/Subject Heading

Indexing is the art of identifying the subjects contained in a given publication and matching these identified subjects with corresponding words/ terms listed in a list of subject headings or in a thesaurus. The terms used in indexing are called subject headings, descriptors or index terms.

As already described in Chapters 4 and 5, indexing and classifying are both parts of subject cataloguing or contents description. Since subject headings are never used for shelving and filing of books and documents, it is necessary to complement subject heading catalogues with a shelf list showing the actual place of books on the shelves. This is not necessary when a classification is used for contents description (see also Chapter 7.2 "Classified Catalogue" and Chapter 7.4 "Subject Heading Catalogue").

The content of any given publication can be described by using many different words/terms, i.e. subject headings. If, for instance, you ask several persons to describe the content of a book on economic development and political change in developing countries by choosing three to five words only, you will probably get as many different answers as persons asked, i.e. Economic Development, Underdevelopment, Economic Theory, Growth Theory, Development, Developing Country, Third World, Politics, Change, Political Change, Industrialization, Dependency, Economics, Dual Economy, etc. Each term/word covers to some extent the content of the book and as you may have noticed some are synonyms. If you choose all possible terms one could think of as subject headings it might perhaps be of some use to the inexperienced user but at the same time it would be confusing as the card catalogue will soon assume alarming proportions and will not be clear and consistent. **Too many overlapping terms are not useful but only confusing.** Nor is it any good to simply invent subject headings. But then how do you proceed? How can one limit the number of possible terms and choose suitable ones?

One step in achieving some consistency in indexing is to use a **controlled vocabulary**, i.e. a subject headings list or a thesaurus. The terms listed in a thesaurus generally are called descriptors.

The best-known English-language subject heading lists are the *Sears List of Subject Headings* and the *Library of Congress Subject Headings List*. And there are hundreds of thesauri for all special fields of knowledge.

6.1 Thesaurus

A thesaurus is a collection of descriptors — generally within one special field of knowledge — which not only lists the terms in alphabetical order but also displays their relationship. Each descriptor is followed, where necessary, by a scope note (SN), i.e. a brief explanation of how it should be used, and references to the synonymous descriptors, i.e. defining which of several possible synonyms should be used (UF — used for). The thesaurus also refers the user to the top term (TT), broader (BT), specific (NT = narrower term) and/or related (RT) descriptors.

The following example is taken from the OECD Macrothesaurus:

Special education
  SN: Special types of education for exceptional (gifted or handicapped) children.
        TT: EDUCATIONAL SYSTEMS
        BT: EDUCATIONAL SYSTEMS
        NT: COMPENSATORY EDUCATION
              CORRECTIONAL EDUCATION
        RT: GIFTED STUDENT
              MENTAL RETARDATION
              SPECIAL SCHOOLS

Thesauri are available for nearly all special fields of knowledge, for instance agriculture, environment, cultural development, labour, industrial development, chemistry, and engineering. In 1985 a "Thesaurus Guide" was published listing the most important thesauri presently available.[1]

If you decide to use subject headings, we recommend the use of the "Macrothesaurus for Information Processing in the Field of Economic and Social Development" which we think is the most appropriate for libraries specializing in appropriate technology and rural development. It was published by the OECD — that is why it is still known as the OECD Thesaurus — but the latest (3rd) edition has been published under the auspices of the United Nations.[2] It is available in English, French, Spanish, Indonesian (based on the 1st edition), and Arabic. You may inquire at the OECD and UN whether further translations are available.

6.2 Assigning Subject Headings

Even with the help of thesauri the assignment of subject headings remains the most difficult task in a library and requires much knowledge and

---

[1] Gesellschaft für Information und Dokumentation (GID): Thesaurus Guide. An analytical directory of selected vocabularies for information retrieval, 1985. For the Commission of the European Communities. Amsterdam: North Holland/Luxembourg: EC 1985. 749 p.

[2] Macrothesaurus for Information Processing in the Field of Economic and Social Development. English — French — Spanish. 3rd ed. Prepared by Jean Viet. New York: United Nations 1985. 347 p.

experience. As it is assumed the target group of this manual does not yet have the training and experience in documentation work which are indispensable requirements for an accurate use of subject headings, **we do not recommend the setting up of a subject heading catalogue from the very beginning.** But you may, of course, consider establishing a subject heading catalogue after having gained some experience and as the need arises. On the question whether to use subject headings for information processing, Herbert H. Hoffman remarks: "... the assignment of subject headings to publications is very difficult work. Like classification, it requires a thorough understanding of the field of knowledge represented by the library's collection. There is no shortcut possible because the task requires two fundamental steps that cannot be simplified. They are,

(1) an examination of the publication to determine what it is about (which takes knowledge and experience), and

(2) the selection of suitable terms to express the subject content in such a way that all publications dealing in a similar way with the same topics will always carry the same subject headings (which takes more knowledge, experience, and a thorough familiarity with the schedule of headings used as well as with the collection).

If the cataloger lacks the subject knowledge and/or necessary experience and cannot enlist the help of an expert it is far better to defer the making of subject added entries, or even abandon the project altogether, than to waste time and energy on the childish exercise of listing a book in a medical library, entitled 'Introduction to Medicine', under the subject heading Medicine ...! Far better not to have a subject catalog than a poorly done subject catalog that will describe books under topics and aspects that they don't really deal with, or fail to describe important publications under the key subjects that they do deal with...[1]"

If you do decide to use subject headings for information processing, you should first study carefully a handbook dealing with the subject (see List of Further Readings at the back). It would go beyond the scope of this manual to explain in detail how to proceed in such a case.

---

[1] Hoffman, Herbert H.: Small Library Cataloging. Santa Ana, Calif.: Headway 1977, p. 95/96.

6.3 Geographical Subject Headings

As also described in Chapter 7.5 (Geographical Catalogue), it might be useful and indeed necessary for some organizations to assign geographical subject headings. In such a case you need geographical descriptors as well as descriptors regarding content. As geographical descriptors you should use only those which are already used by large libraries in your country and/or the Bureau of Statistics. Do not invent your own descriptors!

THE FIRST STEP IS TO DECIDE ON THE DESCRIPTORS TO BE USED. AS IT CAN BE ASSUMED THAT YOU DO NOT HAVE OR NEED A THESAURUS YET, YOU SHOULD USE THE ALPHABETICAL INDEX OF YOUR CLASSIFICATION SCHEME. BUT IN CASE YOU WANT TO INTRODUCE A THESAURUS, THE ABOVE MENTIONED OECD MACROTHESAURUS HAS PROVED TO BE MOST SUITABLE IN MANY CASES.

THE SECOND STEP WILL BE TO CAREFULLY STUDY THE PUBLICATION — ESPECIALLY THE TABLE OF CONTENTS — IN ORDER TO ASCERTAIN THE MAIN SUBJECTS. TAKE NOTES OF THE TERMS YOU THINK WILL BE APPROPRIATE TO COVER THE CONTENT IN THE BEST POSSIBLE WAY.

THE THIRD STEP WILL BE TO COMPARE THE TERMS YOU CHOSE WITH THE DESCRIPTORS LISTED IN THE THESAURUS AND DECIDE ON THE MOST SUITABLE ONES. IF A BOOK DEALS WITH ONE SUBJECT ONLY CHOOSE THE NARROWEST TERM THAT CHARACTERIZES THE SUBJECT.

A library specializing in Sarawak (a province in East Malaysia) should describe the content of a book on the farming practices of the Ibans (a tribe in Sarawak) by using the descriptors SARAWAK/IBAN + SHIFTING CULTIVATION. The broader terms AGRICULTURE and FARMING SYSTEM should not be used as they are not detailed enough to characterize the content in a concise way. Nor would the broader geographical term MALAYSIA be necessary either for a library situated in Malaysia.

The book "Ventilated Improved Pit Latrines: Recent Developments in Zimbabwe" by Peter R. Morgan and D. Duncan Mara will be sufficiently described by the subject headings ZIMBABWE/TOILETS. (The Macrothesaurus recommends the use of the term 'toilet' instead of 'latrines'.) If a book deals with several subjects and/or important sub-topics of a general topic several descriptors should be assigned. The book "China: Recycling of organic wastes in agriculture" is given the descriptors CHINA/ AGRICULTURAL WASTES + BIOGAS + COMPOSTING.

The descriptors will be either typed at the top right-hand corner of the catalogue card or at the very bottom (see Figs. 33 and 34).

In Chapter 5, "Classifying", some general principles of subject cataloguing are already described in a more detailed way. Since the principles and steps involved in classifying can also be applied to subject headings, please refer to that chapter for further information.

Fig. 33: Where to write descriptors/subject headings

```
                          CHINA/ Agricultural Wastes +
                          Biogas + Composting

   14.10
   foo
                 FOOD AND AGRICULTURE ORGANIZATION (FAO)

                 China: Recycling of organic wastes in
                 agriculture. Report of an FAO/UNDP study
                 tour to the People's Republic of China.
                 28 april - 24 may 1977.
                 Rome: FAO 1977. 122 p

                 (FAO Soils Bulletin. 4o)
```

```
14.10
foo        FOOD AND AGRICULTURE ORGANIZATION (FAO)

           China: Recycling of organic wastes in
           agriculture. Report of an FAO/UNDP study
           tour to the People's Republic of China.
           28 apirl - 24 may 1977.
           Rome: FAO 1977. 122 p

           (FAO Soils Bulletin. 4o)

            CHINA/ Agricultural Wastes + Biogas +
                   Composting
```

Fig. 34: *Where to write descriptors/subject headings*

7. Card Catalogues

In a card catalogue, the entries are prepared on standard cards and filed in drawers. They may be arranged by alphabet, number or subject. In all card catalogues, several entries for the same book may be filed according to the various subjects covered and other entries respectively.

The card catalogue is the library's most important reference tool. You therefore should ensure that catalogue cards are never taken out of the drawers as a user will only have complete information on all books available in the library with the help of the catalogues!

For a small library two different types of card catalogues are essential or even compulsory:

— Author Catalogue and
— Classified Catalogue.

Further optional card catalogues are:

— Title Catalogue
— Subject Heading Catalogue
— Geographical Catalogue.

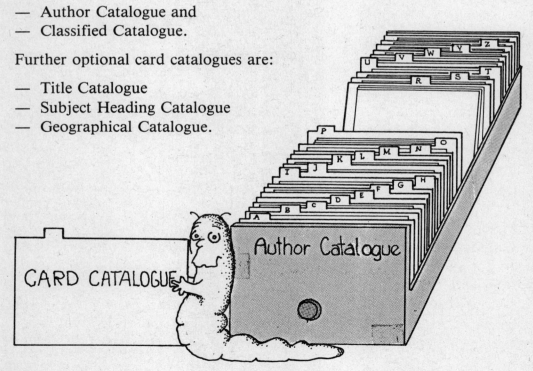

Please remember: No matter which kind of catalogue you decide to create, the card catalogue, as the primary reference source, must be always complete and current. As already emphasized above, only the card catalogues provide access to a particular book by either author, title or subject and refer to the location through the call number.

It is important to check the catalogues from time to time for consistency of classification and to file all necessary guide cards and cross-references.

important remarks

7.1 Author Catalogue

The author catalogue informs the library user and the librarian which works written by a given personal or corporate author are available in the library.

If, for example, a library user asks for books by John Smith, you can only find out whether they are available in your library by looking up 'Smith, John' in the author catalogue. The author catalogue is the main instrument for the librarian to find out whether a work by a given author already exists in the library. It should always be consulted before ordering new books and before cataloguing new additons. In this way you may save a lot of time, money and work.

Filing

Catalogue cards will be arranged in alphabetical order according to author and institution names (and of titles in the case of an anonymous work and if you do not install a title catalogue) together in one alphabet. If there are several entries by the same author, the next filing criterion will be the title. The filing order for titles is alphabetical, word by word arrangement. Please note that initial articles (definite and indefinite) are to be ignored in filing as arrangement criteria since so many titles begin with such an article (in English: "The", "A", and "An"). But, of course, you must not omit the initial articles when typing the catalogue card!

Examples for Filing

Aarsse, A.T.
Abadilla, Domingo C.
Abbatt, F.R.
Abert, James G.
Academy of Gandhian Studies
Appropriate Technology Development Association (ATDA)
  Some developments of appropriate technology ...
Appropriate Technology Development Association (ATDA)
  A study of fibre industry in India.
Appropriate Technology Development Association (ATDA)
  A study of village oil industry in India.
Appropriate Technology Development Institute (ATDI)
  Community-based food processing industries ...
Appropriate Technology Development Institute (ATDI)
  Liklik Buk. A sourcebook for development workers ...
Appropriate Technology Development Institute (ATDI)
  Subsistence fishing practices of Papua New Guinea.
Appropriate Technology Development Organization (ATDO)
  Build your own hydro-electric power plant.
Appropriate Technology Development Organization (ATDO)
  Gobar gas. An alternative way of handling the ...
Appropriate Technology International (ATI)
  Ferrocement fishing boats:
Appropriate Technology International (ATI)
  Selected bibliography on cementious materials.
Aprovecho Institute
Asian Institute of Technology

For title filing rules, see "Title Catalogue" (Chapter 7.3) since the same rules apply for filing several titles by the same author in the author catalogue.

The same authors will be filed differently if you use the acronyms instead of the full name.

Please remember: When you decide to use the acronym of an organization you have to file it in the sequence of the letters.

Aarsse, A.T.
Abadilla, Domingo C.
Abbatt, F.R.
Abel, K.
Abert, James G.
Academy of Gandhian Studies
Aprovecho Institute
Asian Institute of Technology
ATDA
ATDI
ATDO
ATI

7.2 Classified Catalogue

The classified catalogue informs the library user and the librarian which publications on a given subject are available in the library.
The classified catalogue is arranged by subject according to the classification system chosen for your library. The classified catalogue is partly identical with the shelf list as the arrangement of cards corresponds with the arrangement of books on the shelves. A **shelf list** is a record of books in the order in which they stand on the shelves.

If, for example, you want to find out how many and which books on 'organic agriculture' are available in the library, you can do so by checking the respective class in the classified catalogue. This is the only complete listing of all relevant publications available in the library, including the ones presently on loan and also those in which the subject "organic agriculture" is only one of several and which therefore had been assigned the second class number "organic agriculture". On the shelves you will only find relevant books which are presently available, but not the ones which have been borrowed.

You should always remind the users to first search for information in the catalogues instead of going directly to the shelves. Otherwise they will probably miss valuable documents on the subject they are looking for.

Filing

In the classified catalogue, the cards will be arranged according to class numbers. Within one class number cards are filed according to the author's name in alphabetical order. See also the paragraph "Cataloguing and Filing of Catalogue Cards of Nonbook Materials" in Chapter 9.

Examples for filing

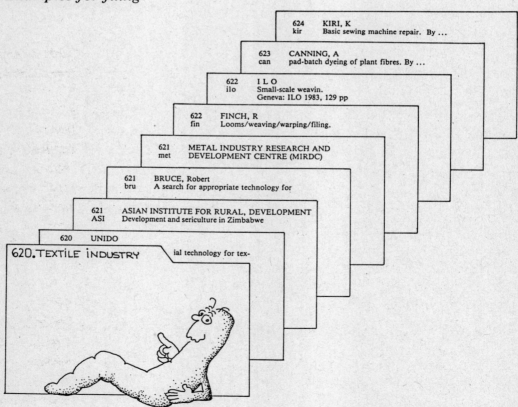

7.3 Title Catalogue

Title catalogues refer the user of a library to the titles of books. They are particularly helpful to those readers who are more likely to remember the title of a publication than its author. Some readers use the title catalogue as a kind of subject catalogue. They are right in assuming that some titles begin with the term they are looking for, i.e. that the titles of quite a number of books on biogas, for instance, begin with the term biogas. Such a search, however, excludes all titles beginning differently. The great problem with title catalogues is that users often do not remember a title correctly. Library users often remember only the key words of a title, but not the correct and complete one. A user might, for instance, insist on borrowing the book entitled 'Food and Farming in the New Nicaragua' which he has already seen in your library but he has forgotten that the proper title of this publication is 'What Difference Could A Revolution Make?' and that what he remembered is the subtitle. In such a case, that book cannot be found as the title entry is, of course, made under its correct title and not under the subtitle. In addition users often do not remember that the publication they are looking for starts with "A report of . . ." or "Study on . . .". That is why the usefulness of title catalogues for small special libraries and documentation centres may be limited although they are widely used in English-speaking countries. In Germany, for instance, title catalogues are popular only in public libraries since a large part of the collection there consists of fiction; and readers of fiction more often remember the title of a novel than its author.

If you decide for one reason or the other to set up a title catalogue, it is not difficult to do so. You simply duplicate one more main entry card and underline the title as an added entry.

Filing

As already mentioned above, correct filing order is an alphabetical, word-by-word arrangement.

The rules listed below for filing should be followed consistently:

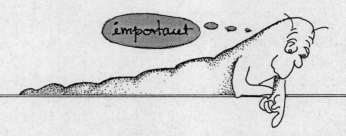

1. Initial articles in all languages (English: A, An, The) will be ignored.
   Example: **Water** and sanitation
            A **water** tank for small communities
            The **water** tanks of Sri Lanka
2. Abbreviations are arranged as spelled in full in the language of the entry.
3. Numerals in titles are arranged as spelled in the language. Example: "1000 new stoves for India" will be filed as if the number had been spelled = "1000 <One thousand> new stoves for India". The title will thus be filed under "One".
4. Words spelled in different ways are interfiled as if spelled in one way. In such a case you should use the spelling common in your country. This rule, for example, is illustrated by differences in American and British spelling, e.g. 'centre' and 'center'.

7.4 Subject Heading Catalogue

A subject heading catalogue (also called subject authority file) **guarantees the easiest access to information on given subjects.**
A subject heading catalogue is based on a list of subject headings or a thesaurus. If handled in an optimal way, it can be regarded as the best reference tool in a library. But it is also more difficult to set up and maintain than any other catalogue.
The technical implementation is quite simple but the assignment of subject headings or terms which indicate the content of a work in the best possible way is difficult and requires time and experience. (For indexing/subject heading see also Chapter 6.)

A subject heading catalogue should only be used if
—the librarian has sufficient understanding of the field (in our case AT) in which the organization works and the special terminology used,
—the librarian has enough time to concentrate on the difficult task of choosing the right subject headings,
—the librarian has sufficient knowledge of the foreign language most widespread in his/her country, and
—the librarian can be sure of the support of his/her colleagues in indexing.

Filing

In a subject heading catalogue, subject entries are arranged in alphabetical order. Within each subject, the filing order may either be done according to the author's name in alphabetical order or according to the date of publication, i.e. the latest one published is filed first.

7.5 Geographical Catalogue

A geographical catalogue provides easy access to information on given provinces, districts, tribes and geographic areas. A geographical catalogue can be part of the subject heading catalogue since a country's, province's or town's name is also a subject heading.
But it is advisable to separate a geographical catalogue from the subject heading catalogue for reasons of clarity. A geographical catalogue can, of course, be installed without a subject heading catalogue. The instalment of a geographical catalogue is strongly recommended for documentation centres specializing not only in appropriate technology, organic agricul-

ture, environment or rural development but also in the collection of publications about a particular country or region.

It depends on the specialization of the respective NGO how detailed geographical subject headings should be. It might not be useful to always include the smallest geographical unit (e.g. village) as a geographical subject heading as there might be villages with the same name in different provinces. But if, for instance, an organization is concentrating on information only about the province where it operates, it might be useful to also use village names as geographical subject headings (see also Chapter 6.3 "Geographical Subject Headings").

Filing
There are two possibilities for the arrangement of cards:
1. The file order is strictly according to alphabetical arrangement of the geographical terms, e.g.

> Agusan del Norte/ ...
> Agusan del Sur/ ...
> Bukidnon/ ...
> Davao/ ...
> Luzon/ ...
> Manila/ ...
> Negros/ ...
> Philippines/ ...
> Zamboanga/ ...

2. The higher political or geographic area is filed first, followed in alphabetical order by the various islands or provinces, e.g.

> Philippines/Economic Situation
> Philippines/Labour Policy
> Philippines/Legislation
> Philippines/Military Bases
> Philippines/Social Conditions
> etc.
> Manila/ ...
> Mindanao, Agusan del Norte/ ...
> Mindanao, Bukidnon/ ...

Mindanao, Davao/ ...
Mindanao, North Cotabatu/ ...
Mindanao, Zamboanga/ ...
etc.
Visayas/ ...
Visayas, Negros Occidental/ ...
Visayas, Negros Oriental/ ...

But it might be as useful to have 'Negros' (the name of an island, not of a province), for instance, as an independent entry in the regional catalogue. You are the best judge!

7.6 Catalogue Maintenance

A small documentation centre will need a minimum of two card catalogues (author and classified catalogues) and a maximum of five catalogues (author, classified, title, geographical and subject heading catalogue). A **catalogue cabinet** with several drawers is needed. (For details see Chapter 14 "Furniture and Equipment".)
The drawers (also called 'trays') should be near eye level so that they can be easily reached. It is better to have fewer drawers per vertical row and to spread them in width. Thus, more persons can use the catalogue at the same time.

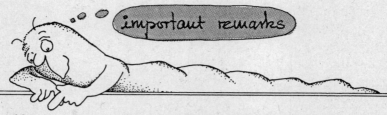

Even if you start very small, there should be always **one drawer for each type of catalogue.** Never put different catalogues into one drawer.

In the beginning, drawers should only be one-third or half full in order to provide space for expansion.

While planning the amount of drawers needed you should make sure that there are at least two spare drawers for later expansion.

You will be surprised how fast you will need them. In estimating the size of the catalogue cabinet, i.e. how many drawers you will need, one may figure a thousand cards to a drawer and five cards for each title.

A drawer can already be regarded full when it is filled up to approx. 80%. If more cards are put in it will be difficult to push the cards back and forth so that one can read the whole card.

Each drawer is to be labelled showing the content of that drawer, e.g. Author Catalogue A—K, Author Catalogue L—Z, Classified Catalogue 01.00—09.00, Classified Catalogue 10.00—18.00, Classified Catalogue 19.00—21.00.

You will also need **guide cards** (also called catalogue dividers). Guide cards are inserted in a card catalogue to help the user find a desired place or heading in the catalogue. They are slightly higher than the catalogue cards and are made of strong cardboard or plastic. For the author and title catalogues you will need **A—Z guides.** For the other catalogues it is best to use half-cut guide cards and alternate right- and left-hand tabs. Maximum clarity is achieved by labelling the guide cards carefully with the class number and the title of the class (full if possible, otherwise abridged).

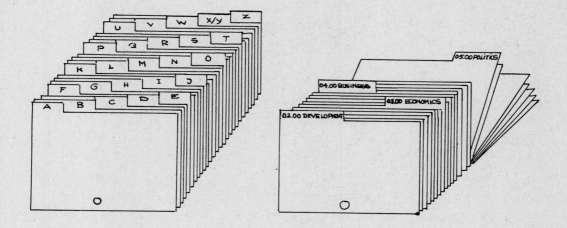

If you cannot purchase guide cards ready made, you can make them your-self by pasting three cards together; the one in the middle should project about 1 cm. You then cut half of the projection. You could also try to obtain reinforced cardboard and have the guide cards cut by a print shop.

It is important to check the catalogues from time to time for con-sistency of classification and to file all necessary guide cards and cross-references.

8. Foreign Language Books

Many NGOs in the Third World receive and need publications not only in their particular national language(s) but also in foreign languages. In fact, the proportion of foreign language publications often amounts to up to 50% of the total collection, and can be even higher.

As long as the respective foreign language is widespread and the national language(s) use(s) the characters of the Roman alphabet, the problems arising are manageable. First of all it is a problem for librarians. Even if they master the foreign language, it nevertheless is more difficult and takes more time to classify foreign language materials than books in their mother tongue. And, of course, it is also a problem for those users who have difficulty in reading the respective foreign language but who need information on a topic where no publications or only a few are available in their own language. In such a case they will need translation support and guidance by the librarian and/or staff members.

For a librarian it is indispensable to at least have a basic command of the foreign language most widespread in his/her country (for most readers of this manual it will be English). Otherwise it is impossible to correctly classify library materials. If you are not sure whether you understand the meaning of a title, do not hesitate to ask colleagues who are more fluent in the respective language for help in classifying the book. It is always easier to ask for help beforehand than to correct mistakes afterwards.

For **cataloguing foreign language books** the same rules as described in Chapter 3 are applied. And the arrangement of books on the shelves follows the same order regardless of language, i.e. books on the same subject but in different languages are placed together.

Before ordering any foreign language books you should consider whether the majority of your users will be able to read them. From time to time your organization will probably receive foreign language publications free of charge from other organizations or from colleagues returning from trips abroad. As long as these publications are written in a language most library users are familiar with, you may add them to your collection. But it becomes a problem if they are written in a language the majority of library users and staff members do not understand. What should you do with such publications? It is pointless to keep books which nobody will ever read, but they might be useful to others!

Here are three possibilities to dispose of them:

1. Offer them to your colleagues and/or users for their own personal collection.
2. Submit them to the nearest university library or your National Library, or any other library specializing in the respective subject area.
3. Simply throw them away. (This applies particularly to international conference papers which usually are published in several languages. If the subject is important to you, try to obtain copies in a language with which you are familiar and discard other versions.)

For more information regarding acquisition policy, see Chapter 12 "Acquisition".

8.1 Publications in a Non-Roman Script

If your national language uses a non-Roman script such as Arabic, Chinese, Hindi, Singhalese, Tamil, or Thai, you should split your collection into two separate sections within the library — one for each language. Such a step is recommended in order to keep the library clearly laid out. Because of the different scripts, catalogue cards and call numbers have to be typed in different ways. Therefore you will need two card catalogues, for example:

author catalogue (Thai)
author catalogue (English)
classified catalogue (Thai)
classified catalogue (English).

The books should also be set apart on the shelves. Although the author of his manual is not familiar with any of the abovementioned languages, it can be presumed that cataloguing is done according to different rules. You will probably be able to obtain the cataloguing rules which apply to your country/language from your national library association or your National Library. Additionally, the reader is referred to the book "Cataloging and Classification of Non-Western Material: Concerns, Issues and Practices. Edited by Mohammed M. Aman". Its 12 chapters deal with the following countries/regions/languages: Nigeria, Ghana, Africa, Chinese, Japanese, Southeast Asia, India, Pakistan, Arabic, Slavic, Hebraic.

9. Nonbook Materials

An information explosion has been with us for several decades. Not only are more and more books being published each year but there is also a tremendous increase in the production of nonbook materials.

Nonbook materials consist of periodicals, newspapers, pamphlets, maps, photographs, pictures, posters, slides, film strips, motion pictures, video tapes, cassettes, microfilms and microfiches, computer disks, etc.

Today, as an information service, a library is not effective if it does not make some of these materials available to its users. It is also assumed that NGOs worldwide receive some of the above mentioned materials which is why they have to be dealt with here too.

Accessions book for nonbook materials
Except for periodicals, pamphlets and clippings, all nonbook materials should be entered into an accessions book. In order not to mix up books and documents with nonbook materials, start a separate accessions book with separate sections for different materials, for example:

- photographs (Ph)
- slides (S)
- video tapes (V)
- motion pictures/films (F)
- sound recordings (C)
- microfiches and/or microfilms (M)
- posters (Po).

In each section the accession number starts with 1 and will be preceded by the symbol (the capital letter shown above in brackets) for the specific kind of material. The 21st tape or audio cassette in your library will thus receive the number C-21.

For the above listed nonbook materials the accession number serves both location and arrangement purposes.

Storage of nonbook materials

The storage of nonbook materials differs greatly from that of books. They often require special treatment and storage facilities such as vertical files, hanging/suspending files, specially designed cabinets, shelves and boxes. Safe storage of some nonbook materials (e.g. films, video tapes, motion pictures, disks) require a special atmosphere. Humidity, dryness and temperature should be such that they do not damage the materials. In the following paragraphs it is possible to give only general guidelines and hints. For advice on how best to store and protect your materials you should inquire locally.

Cataloguing and filing of catalogue cards of nonbook materials

Generally, most nonbook materials are catalogued according to the same rules applied to books. For details see the following chapters.

But there are differences in **filing** the catalogue cards. The cards of those materials to which you assigned a class number should, of course, be filed in the classified catalogue. The call number for nonbook materials differs from the one for books, and therefore it is advisable to place the catalogue cards for nonbook materials at the very end of each class (Fig. 35). If you have a considerable number of catalogued nonbook materials in your library it is advisable to reserve one drawer of your catalogue cabinet

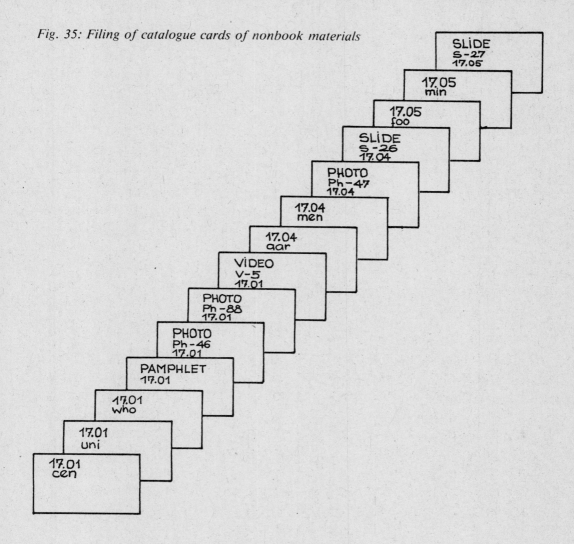

Fig. 35: Filing of catalogue cards of nonbook materials

for the cards of nonbook materials and to file the catalogue cards according to the kind of materials in numerical order of accession numbers, e.g. Cassette/C-1 to Cassette/C-14 or Photo/Ph-1 to Photo/Ph-78. Do not forget to insert guide cards and to label the drawer appropriately.

If there are author and title cards for nonbook materials they should be filed together with the catalogue cards for books in the respective card catalogues.

With regard to the title catalogue please remember that there is no sense in preparing a catalogue card for a title which you invented as will be the case with photographs, slides, pamphlet files, etc.

9.1 Periodicals

The term periodical includes journals, magazines, and newsletters (except daily ones, i.e. newspapers) which are published consecutively and at regular intervals. Periodicals are an important source of information for all documentation centres as they are more current and up to date than books. In the field of rural development and appropriate technology, there are many periodicals which may be obtained free of charge.[1] But be careful not to collect too many. Before ordering any new periodical, give it though and discuss the matter with your colleagues. Take into account that time and space are needed to make full use of these periodicals.

For each periodical a **record card** (also called 'checking card') is used to enter each issue as it is received. The record card should be 15 cm × 21 cm. By using a fairly large size it can be used for many volumes or years. Any local printer can print such cards but you can also make them yourself if you do not need more than about 20 copies (see Fig. 37). The back of the card should be left blank for notes, e.g.

— How long will the periodical be kept? (indefinitely, 5/4/3/2/1 years, current issue only)
— If kept indefinitely complete volume to be bound? yes/no
— Display on the display shelf? yes/no
— To whom will it be circulated regularly? (circulation list)

The record cards are kept in a separate card tray and filed in alphabetical order by title.

Generally, periodicals are not catalogued and classified since the record card already exists. Important articles should be photocopied and filed in the respective pamphlets file (see also: pamphlets).

If you do not want to photocopy the article you can also refer the user directly to the article by preparing a reference card for the catalogue (Fig. 36). The user will thus know that he will find the article in the journal "The Courier" and not on the shelves.

In exceptional cases, a special number of a journal which treats a single subject of importance to your library can be treated as a monograph, i.e. catalogued and classified, and put on the shelves. In such a case, it is ad-

---

[1]   A list of periodicals (around 120 items) received by GATE's documentation centre can be obtained free of charge from GATE on request.

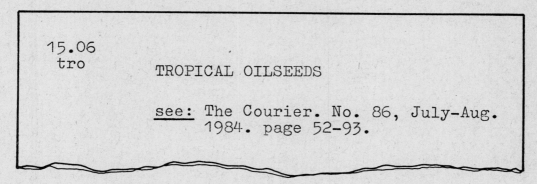

```
15.06
tro                  TROPICAL OILSEEDS

                     see: The Courier. No. 86, July-Aug.
                          1984. page 52-93.
```

Fig. 36: Cataloguing periodicals

visable to photocopy the title page, note down the call number and file it in the respective magazine box to avoid a search for that specific number.

Storage of periodicals

Periodicals are best stored in a specially designed box called a 'magazine box' or a 'pamphlet file'. Newsletters which come without a cover and consist of a few pages only are best stored in loose-leaf binders as they crumple easily if put into boxes. The periodicals are stamped with ownership, put into boxes or files and arranged in alphabetical order by title in a special section of the shelves. Each box/file should be clearly marked with the title and the volume(s) it contains.

See the following pages for a sample for record cards (size: 15 × 21 cm).

Figs. 37a – d: Record card for periodicals

TITLE								weekly/monthly/bimonthly
PUBLISHER								quarterly/twice a year
SUPPLIER								PRICE:

YEAR	VOL	Jan	Feb	Mar	Apr	May	June	July	Aug	Sep	Oct	Nov	Dec	Suppl

TITLE WINDPOWER MONTHLY NEWS MAGAZINE								weekly/(monthly)/bimonthly
PUBLISHER FORLAGET VISTOFT APS, URINNERS HOVED DK 8420 KNEBEL DENMARK								quarterly/twice a year
SUPPLIER dto								PRICE: US $ Airmail 35.70

YEAR	VOL	Jan	Feb	Mar	Apr	May	June	July	Aug	Sep	Oct	Nov	Dec	Suppl
1985	1	✓	✓	✓	✓	missing	✓	✓	✓	✓	✓	✓	✓	
1986	2	✓	✓	✓	✓	✓	✓	✓	✓	✓	✓			
1987	3			✓						✓				

TITLE **THE COURIER**
AFRICA - CARIBBEAN - PACIFIC - EUR. COMMUNITY weekly/monthly/(bimonthly)
quarterly/twice a year
PUBLISHER Commission of the European
Communities, Brussels / Belgium
SUPPLIER dto
PRICE: free

YEAR	VOL	Jan	Feb	Mar	Apr	May	June	July	Aug	Sep	Oct	Nov	Dec	Suppl
1987		101 24.2.87		102 1.5.			103 30.6.		104 5.9.	105 10.11.		106 5.1.88		
1988		107 1.3.88												
					In this case the publisher did not assign individual numbers for each volume but numbered the various issues consecutively.								

TITLE **APPROPRIATE TECHNOLOGY** weekly/monthly/bimonthly
(quarterly)/twice a year
PUBLISHER ITDG 9, King Street
London, U.K.
SUPPLIER IT Publications
PRICE: £ 12.00 p.a.

YEAR	VOL	Jan	Feb	Mar	Apr	May	June	July	Aug	Sep	Oct	Nov	Dec	Supp
1984/85	11			4 28.3.85			1 15.6.84			2 10.9.84		3 8.12.84		
1985/86	12			4 19.3.86			1 10.6.85			2 13.9.85		3 16.12.85		
1986/87	13			4 20.4.87			1 2.7.86			2 30.9.86		3 4.1.86		
					Publication of this journal started with No.1 in June — and not in January as you would expect.								

9.2 Pamphlets

The definition of a pamphlet is first of all based on its form, i.e. that it is a printed work not permanently bound. Pamphlets often provide more up-to-date information than books.

Some pamphlets may have permanent value (and a considerable number of pages) even if unbound. In such a case, the pamphlet should be bound and treated as a book, i.e. catalogued, classified, provided with a call number and put on the shelves.

All others which are either too thin (a few pages only) or too insignificant to be kept permanently will most probably consist of:

— important articles from journals,
— short project reports or other project documents,
— leaflets about specific products and plants for instance,
— leaflets about organizations,
— or any other unbound material.

And sometimes it can be useful to photocopy important letters and include them in the pamphlets file, for instance the answers to enquiries your organization has sent to the question-and-answer service of organizations abroad.

Pamphlets do not receive an accession number and usually they are not catalogued. Although no catalogue cards will be prepared for them, you nevertheless have to decide on a subject area in order to file them correctly in the pamphlets files. The documents are stamped with ownership and marked with the class number. The class number is preceded by "PAMPHLET". The pamphlets are then put in the **pamphlet file.** The pamphlet file can have the form of a loose-leaf binder or of a magazine box. It depends on the amount of pamphlets you are likely to receive whether you prepare pamphlet files for the respective macro-class number only or whether you assign them specific class numbers, too.

When you start setting up your library it might be sufficient to install one file only for all pamphlets within a given macro-group. But each pamphlet is nevertheless thoroughly classified, i.e. if required down to the third level — but not catalogued!

If you later find out that it will be more appropriate to also have pamphlet files for some main groups you still can divide the file. *Example:* One pamphlet file has been set up for the entire group 05.00 "politics, Public Administration, Law and Legislation". After some time you discover that it is better to have a separate file for "Human Rights". You simply take out those pamphlets dealing with human rights from the general politics file and put them into the new file on human rights. No changes are needed on the catalogue cards (if the pamphlets have been catalogued) since the documents have already been classified with "05.04 — Human Rights".

For each pamphlet file a **list of contents** should be prepared and pasted to the back of the front cover. It is useful to number the pamphlets within each file.

For each pamphlet file one catalogue card only will be prepared and filed in the classified card catalogue, for example:

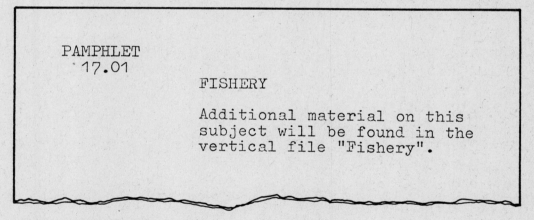

```
PAMPHLET
  17.01

        FISHERY

        Additional material on this
        subject will be found in the
        vertical file "Fishery".
```

Fig. 38: Cataloguing pamphlets

Some of the pamphlets which are not to be bound but which are put in the pamphlets file should nevertheless be catalogued if they are of major importance to your library. They should be catalogued and classified as described in Chapters 3 and 5. But the call number is again preceded by "PAMPHLET" in order to refer the user to its location, i.e. the pamphlet file.

```
  PAMPHLET              ZAMBIA / Women + Food Pro-
  06.04                 duction + Family Planning

                 MILIMO, Mabel C.

                 Women, population and food in Africa:
                 The Zambian case.

                 from: Development. Seeds of change.
                       1987. No. 2/3. p-70-83.
```

Fig. 39: Cataloguing pamphlets

The catalogue cards will be filed together with the catalogue cards for books.

Another way to store pamphlets is by using hanging files (also called suspending files) which are labelled with the responding class number. The advantage of hanging files is that they save space and that storage and filing are a little faster since the documents do not have to be punched.

The disadvantage is that they are more expensive than loose-leaf binders and that you also need a hanging file cabinet. Another disadvantage is that the pamphlets are thus separated from the books which means the user has to search in two different locations for relevant information. Since some of the pamphlets are of temporary value only to your library you should weed the files at regular intervals (once a year should be sufficient) and take out all those which are no longer needed.

9.3 Newspaper Clippings

Clippings/cuttings from newspapers are an important source of information for any documentation centre. They are particularly important for units specializing in collecting information about their own country since **information on current developments of a country generally is first published in newspapers.**

The newspapers to which your organization subscribes are to be checked regularly for articles of possible relevance to your organization's work. As it can be presumed that most of the staff members will also read the newspapers, you should ask them to mark articles to be cut out and kept. At regular intervals (ideally once a week) you should cut out the marked articles and add the source (the newspaper's name) and the date. Be sure to cut out the complete article — quite often articles are continued on another page and one can easily forget to cut that part too. The clippings are then glued on a sheet of paper (again: do not forget to add the source and the date) and sorted according to their main subject. The class number or the subject, e.g. "Transport", "Environment", "Solar Energy", "Pollution Control", "General Election", or "Political Partie" are then written at the top of the sheet.

Clippings may be either stored in a specifically marked section of the pamphlets file or stored separately in hanging files. Once a year the files should be checked and all clippings no longer needed should be weeded out.

If you maintain a fairly large clipping service, it is useful to have stamps with the name of the newspaper. It makes your work easier, faster and tidier.

9.4 Maps

Maps are another important source of information. They come in many different forms: small or large flat maps, wall maps, and folded maps (such as travel or road maps). If possible you should fold the flat maps in such a way that they fit into boxes the size of the magazine boxes.

The area covered is the most important and primary approach; therefore it is recommended that maps be entered under the area covered.

If a map has both geographical and subject aspects, the geographical aspect is regarded as the principal one. The main heading will thus be the area covered. The subject aspect is regarded as secondary and will thus be covered by a secondary class number.

Example: A geologic map of Nepal will be placed by a Nepalese library with 01.03.01/NEP, the secondary class number will be 10.07 (= Geology).

The Rural Development Classification Model provides one class "01.03" for maps. If you have maps of your country and other parts of the world as well, you can subdivide the class for maps as follows:

01.03   Maps, Atlases (world and/or continents)
   01.03.01   Maps, Atlases of . . . (here follows the name of your country)
   01.03.02   Maps, Atlases of other countries

110

In the case of maps, the call number is composed of the class number and the first three letters of the area covered typed in capital letters to distinguish it from the call number for books.

01.03	(= class number)
NEP	(= first three letters of the area covered)

} = call number

In **cataloguing** the following information should be given:

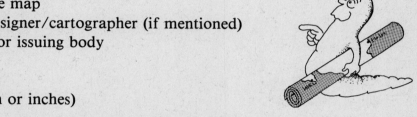

1. Call number
2. Area covered (in capital letters)
3. Title of the map
4. Author/designer/cartographer (if mentioned)
5. Publisher or issuing body
6. Date
7. Scale
8. Size (in cm or inches)

For examples of how to catalogue maps see Figs. 40 + 41.

Fig. 40: Cataloguing maps

```
01.03
  YEM        YEMEN ARAB REPUBLIC

06.06        Administrative division and land use
             in the Yemen Arab Republic. By Urs
11.01        Geier and Hans Steffen. Produced for
             the Swiss Technical Co-operation Ser-
             vice, Bern and the Central Planning
             Organization, San'a. May 1977. Arabic
             and English. (incl. demographic figures
             1:500,000    87 x 115 cm
                              acc.-no
```

```
01.03
MAN
          MANILA

          City map of Manila and suburbs. Covers:
          City of Manila, Makati, Pasay City,
          parts of Caloocan City, Quezon City,
          Mandaluyong. (incl. street index).
          Cartogr. Design: H. Engeler.
          1:12,500. On the back: Metro Manila,
          scale 1:250,000.
          Manila: National Bookstore 1982.
          72.5 x 102 cm
```

Fig. 41: Cataloguing maps

9.5 Photographs

Photographs of the project area, the target group and the work in progress are important aids for the documentation of project activities. In order to provide the users with the best possible information these photos should also be included in the library's collection which means that they are to be catalogued.

The sets of photographs (in exceptional cases single photographs) will be entered in the accessions book for nonbook materials in the form shown in Fig. 42. The entry should contain a note whether the negatives are also available. The same number should always be assigned to the set of photographs and the negatives.

In order to easily distinguish the catalogue cards for photographs from the ones for books and documents the code "Photo" is added to the call number:

```
Photo
Ph-35
```

The call number for photographs is thus composed of the word "Photo" and the accession number only.

112

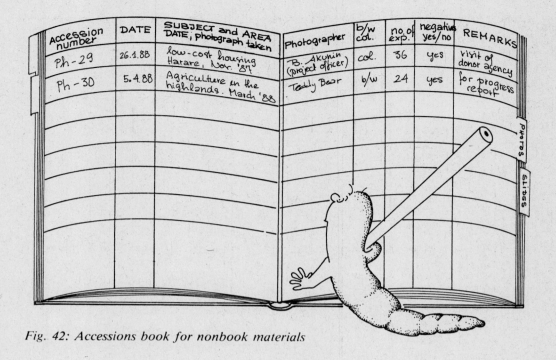

Accession number	DATE	SUBJECT and AREA DATE, photograph taken	Photographer	b/w col.	no. of exp.	negative yes/no	REMARKS
Ph-29	26.1.88	low-cost housing Harare, Nov. '87	B. Akunin (project officer)	col.	36	yes	visit of donor agency
Ph-30	5.4.88	Agriculture in the highlands. March '88	Teddy Bear	b/w	24	yes	for progress report

Fig. 42: Accessions book for nonbook materials

With photographs, the subject area covered is probably more important to the user than the geographical area, and therefore the main heading will be the subject. As photographs do not come with a fixed title you either invent one, simply choose the main subject as the title or use the name of the project as the title. The physical description of photographs includes the following elements:

1. Title/subject
2. Photographer (if known)
3. Short description (area and subjects covered)
4. Date
5. Number in a set
6. Size
7. Black and white or colour (b/w or col.)
8. Accession number

For an example of how to catalogue photographs see Fig. 43.

```
              Irian Jaya, Doromena /
              Drinking Water
 Photo
 Ph-35        CLEAN WATER FOR DOROMENA

 12.o5        Photographs taken during the 3rd
              phase of the project. Installation
              of pipes. Photos taken by Cliff
              Marlessy. May 1985.
              (3o photographs in a set) 9 x 13, b/w
```

Fig. 43: Cataloguing photographs

Storage

Before storing the photographs the location, subject and date should be noted on the back of each photograph (preferably by the photographer himself/herself!). It is advisable to mount them on mounting board or plain white paper; the location, subject and date should be written on the mounting board.

In small collections, i.e. if it is more or less the exception to have photographs and photographic documentation is usually done with slides, photographs are best filed in the appropriate pamphlets file (the file that corresponds with the class number).

But if many photographs are kept, a special photograph file may be established. You can either put them in hanging files or in envelopes which will be kept in steel cabinets or store them in small albums which are provided free of charge in some countries by photo shops. In all cases the storage unit (file/envelope/album) should be marked with the call number, the subject and the date and arranged by accession number.

Negatives, i.e. the roll of developed film, cannot be stored in the same place as the photographs. The negatives should be stored in a cool and dark place, preferably in a steel cabinet, and arranged in numerical order according to accession number.

9.6 Slides

Slides are usually kept in slide trays or transparent slide wallets and stored separately from books in cabinets. They are generally entered under the title which sometimes you might have to invent. Slides are also entered in the accessions book, the accession number is preceded by an "S". For cataloguing and storage see also Chapter 9.5 "Photographs".

```
                              Tanzania / Sisal
        Slide
        S-41      SISAL PRODUCTION  (Slides)

                  Sisal production in the Tanga region /
        15.13     Tanzania. Prepared by TSC.
                  50 slides, col., 5 x 5 cm
```

Fig. 44: Cataloguing slides (fictitious example)

Sound and slide shows which generally consist of a set of slides and an accompanying audio cassette or tape should be entered under slides, as it can be presumed that the slides are more important than the cassette/tape.

Fig. 45: Cataloguing a sound and slide show

```
        Slide
        S- 22     PROJECT RECONSTRUCTION SAIGHANCHI
                  AFGHANISTAN  (Slides)

        21.07     Earthquake resisting building system.
                  Produced by Australian Council of
                  Churches et al. (1980 ?)
                  80 slides, col., 5 x 5 cm
                  1 cassette, 60 min.
```

9.7 Sound Recordings

As it can be assumed that in a small library the majority of recordings , if there are any at all, consist of audio cassettes (folk songs, lectures, interviews, etc.), we will only deal with them and not with phonodiscs although there are only slight differences in cataloguing.

Again, all cassettes should be entered in the special section for cassettes in the accessions book. They are best arranged by accession number and kept in a display tray or any suitable box which then is stored in four-drawer cabinets or any other cabinet.

In cataloguing cassettes the following information should be given:

1. Title
2. Author, i.e. composer and/or singer, lecturer
3. Publisher
4. Date (if available)
5. Stereo or mono
6. Playing time in minutes

There are no fixed rules for sound recordings as to which element is to be regarded as the main heading. It can be the composer, the interpreter (singer, vocalist, soloist, or orchestra) or the title. You should decide yourself how to enter a cassette, depending on where the users will expect to find it.

For examples of how be catalogue cassettes see Fig. 46 + 47.

Fig. 46: Cataloguing cassettes (music)

```
Cassette
C- 56        MAMBESAK

06.12        Seri lagu-lagu rakyat "Iriani".
             Vol. 1 (Irianese folksongs)
             Jayapura: Lembaga Antropologi/UNCEN
             1979.  6o min.
```

```
Cassette
C - 73      MANANZAN, Mary John Sr

            Women and technology. An outline.
06.04       Recording of a lecture given in
            July 1986 during the Intern. Consul-
            tation "Toward A Common Sharing Of
            Technology" in Manila / Philippines.
            Manila: SEARICE 1986.  6o min.
```

Fig. 47: Cataloguing cassettes (lecture)

9.8 Video Tapes and Motion Pictures (Films)

Video tapes and motion pictures/films are entered under their title, followed by the subtitle and the designation "Video" or "Motion Picture".
On the catalogue card the following information will be given:

1. Title and subtitle
2. Sponsor
3. Producer
4. Director
5. Date
6. Running time in minutes (min.)
7. Number of reels or cassettes
8. Indication of sound (sd) or silent (si)
9. Indication of colour (col.) or black and white (b/w)
10. Width in mm
11. Technical system or trade name (for videos only)

For an example of how to catalogue a video tape see Fig. 48.
For an example of how to catalogue a motion picture see Fig. 49.

```
Video
V - 5        SHEA BUTTER PROCESSING IN MALI (Video)

             Sponsor: German Appropriate Technology
15.06        Exchange (GATE), Eschborn.  Director:
             Peter Spielmann.
             1986. 1 cassette, 34 min., sd, col.,
             VHS
```

Fig. 48: Cataloguing a video tape

```
Film
F-6          THE SWEET STINGER. (Motion picture)

             On the beekeeping project Boabeng-Fiema,
16.10        Ghana.) Sponsor: German Appropriate
             Technology Exchange (GATE). Producer:
             N.A.F.T.I. (Ghana Film Institute).
             Director: Mr. Frimpong - Boakye.
             1987. 1 reel, 32 min, sd, col., 16 mm
```

Fig. 49: Cataloguing a motion picture

The accession number of a video tape is preceded by a "V" and the call
number by "VIDEO", for example:

VIDEO
V-6

The accession number of a motion picture/film is preceded by an "F"
and the call number by "FILM", for example:

FILM
F-2

Video tapes and motion pictures are arranged by accession number. They
should be stored in multi-drawer cabinets. Humidity should not be too

118

high as otherwise the films will be damaged by fungus and mould. On the other hand, excessive dryness causes films to curl and become brittle.

9.9 Posters and Charts

For educational purposes some organizations keep posters and charts (flipcharts). When cataloguing these materials the following elements should be included:

1. Author/editor
2. Title/subject (incl. short description)
3. Place of publication
4. Publisher
5. Date of publication
6. Size
7. Black and white or colour

For a fictitious example of how to catalogue posters see Fig. 50.

The easiest and cheapest way to store posters and charts is to roll them up and to keep the rolls in boxes. But there are also flat file cabinets specially designed for oversized materials.

Fig. 50: Cataloguing posters

```
Poster
Po - 4
            WORLD HEALTH ORGANIZATION (WHO)

            Common medicinal plants in Sri Lanka.
13.07.02    Set of posters.
            Colombo: WHO 1986. 3 sheets, 84 x 120 cm
            col.
```

9.10 Microfiche/Computer Disks

As small libraries are more likely to keep microfiches than microfilms, if at all, we will deal solely with microfiches. Microfiches are catalogued according to the rules for the material of which they are a reproduction, i.e. books, periodicals or pamphlets. But the designation "Microfiche" is added to the title and in the collation area mention should be made of the number of cards/microfiches. The accession number is preceded by an "M". If your library has the original document, reference should be made on the catalogue card for the book that a microfiche copy is also available; and on the catalogue card for the microfiche that the original document is available in the library.

It is advisable to store microfiches in boxes specially designed for this purpose. The microfiche supplier will be able to tell you where to obtain these storage boxes.

Computer disks and software programs should only be catalogued if your library has a significant collection of documents in this medium. But they nevertheless are mentioned here since they constitute a new form of storing information. It is self-evident that disks should be carefully labelled and stored. A variety of disk files/boxes are available on the market which protect them from dust and office mishaps. It is advisable to buy ones which can be locked.

10. Preparation and Reproduction of Cards

As your materials are eventually catalogued and classified, you still have to prepare the actual catalogue cards. If you have closely followed the steps described in the previous chapters, you now should have manuscript catalogue cards containing all information for the bibliographic and content description of the documents/books in your collection.

First of all you should decide **how** you are going to reproduce/duplicate the cards.

10.1 Reproduction of Cards

For small libraries there are several ways to reproduce or duplicate cards.

Typing

All cards are typed separately, i.e. the main entry card and the various added entry cards are to be typed. If this method is chosen, you only need a typewriter which is, of course, a great advantage to small organizations. But the disadvantage is that spelling mistakes can easily slip in and that it generally takes more time. An extremely thorough proofreading of each copy is needed. A spelling mistake in the author's name can have serious consequences, e.g. that the book cannot be retrieved in the author catalogue.

Using a duplicator

There are three techniques — spirit duplicating, stencil duplicating and offset printing — which require different machines. **Spirit duplicating** is not recommended — though it is economical and easy to handle — because the ink quickly fades when exposed to light.

For small libraries which only need a small number of copies **offset printing** is not recommended either as the machines are quite expensive. Offset printing should only be considered if the parent organization already has an offset printer.

The most appropriate technique for small libraries in the Third World is **stencil duplicating.** Stencil duplicators utilize a master copy and a stencil. The letters are cut into the stencil and the ink is squeezed through and deposited on the paper. For a small information unit a manually operated duplicator is sufficient. To the author's knowledge there is only one such machine which is produced and distributed by Gaylord Library Supplies, USA (for address and price see chapter "Equipment and Furniture"). This machine is extremely durable and economical and therefore appropriate to small libraries. Although it is not the policy of the author to recommend any particular make, an exception is made in this case as, to her knowledge, the above duplicator is the only one available of its kind. If this process is chosen, first the master copy will be typed on a stencil which then will be duplicated after having been proofread. The duplicator is very simple to operate and can be mastered in a matter of 15 minutes.

Photocopying

Cards can also be photocopied. In such a case, the unit cards are first typed on normal paper the size of the catalogue cards, then proofread, and eventually sorted according to the number of copies needed. Four cards can be photocopied at the same time in case you decide to use the size 10.5 × 14.8 cm. The photocopies then have to be cut and glued on cardboard cards. Reproduction of catalogue cards by photocopying is rather expensive, time-consuming and labour-intensive. Reproduction of cards by photocopying should be chosen only if there is no alternative.

Computerized reproduction

If your organization already has an electronic word processing unit (a personal computer, and a printer), this may be used for printing the catalogue cards. But before making such a decision you should take into account that it is a) quite expensive as you need imported continuous catalogue cards and b) you may not have access to the computer and printer whenever you need them since they will probably be used by your colleagues as well. If you choose this alternative, it is advisable to consult an expert beforehand since some special programming is needed.

10.2 Preparation of Cards

Before finally filing the cards into the card catalogue drawers, several steps are involved:

1. Typing the unit card, the master copy or the stencil.

    Instructions for typing
    The main heading (author or title) begins on about the fourth line from the top of the card and about 12 spaces from the left-hand margin. If the main heading is an author the surname only is typed in capital letters. If the main heading is the title and it needs more than one line, only the first line will be typed in capital letters.
    One line is left between the main heading and title. Subtitle, author information, number of volumes and edition follow consecutively.
    The imprint always begins on a new line.
    The collation follows the imprint consecutively.
    Start a new line for the accession number. The accession number should be typed at the end of this line, not at the beginning.
    On a new line again, the series and series number which should always be typed in brackets are added.

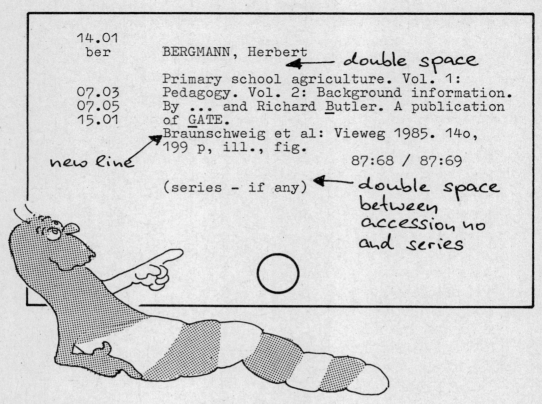

Fig. 51: Sample of how to type a catalogue card

The call number has its place at the top left-hand corner of the catalogue card. Below the call number the secondary class numbers, if any, are typed.

2. Proofreading — a very important step!
3. Determining the number of copies needed. The number of copies depends on
   a) which catalogues are to be installed. Assuming an author catalogue, a title catalogue a classified catalogue and a geographical catalogue will be established, a minimum of four cards are needed.
   b) number of authors/editors. A minimum of 1 (one), and a maximum of 5 (five) cards are needed (3 authors, 2 editing institutions).
   c) title (1 card)

d) series yes/no (1 card)

e) number of class numbers (a minimum of 1 (one) and a maximum of 5 (five)).

In our example the total number of copies needed is 8

(4 class numbers, 2 authors, 1 editing institution, 1 title).

4. Duplicating/reproducing.

5. Marking/underlining. The various entry elements should be underlined on the different copies in red or highlighted with a textliner in order to make sorting and filing easier. First the call number and the secondary class numbers if any are underlined, then the author(s), series and geographical heading if any. Remember that each entry is underlined/marked on a separate card (see Fig. 52).

6. Sorting of catalogue cards. Immediately after having underlined/marked the various entries you should do a rough sorting according to the different catalogues, i.e. put the cards in piles for each of the various catalogues. Then the cards can be filed in alphabetical order for the author catalogue, the series, and the geographical catalogue, and in numerical order for the classified catalogue.

7. Filing the cards into the catalogue card drawers according to the rules described in Chapter 7 "Card Catalogues".

10.3 Size of Catalogue Card

Worldwide, two different sizes of catalogue cards are in general use. Large libraries, e.g. university libraries, generally use the standard size 12.5 cm × 7.5 cm particularly in order to save space. Others, including many documentation centres and most SATIS members, use the larger standard size 14.8 cm × 10.5 cm. If you use the larger size, you will have more space to provide users with additonal information.

It is advisable to use catalogue cards uniformly cut and punched with a hole in the lower centre. You can purchase them ready made or made to order locally. Thus, cards can be secured with the rod in the drawers from accidentally falling out and/or being taken out by unauthorized persons.

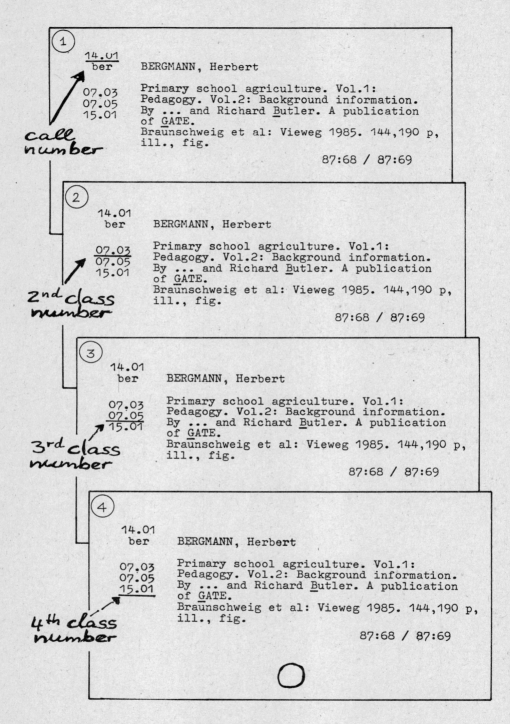

Fig. 52: Marking/underlining the various entries

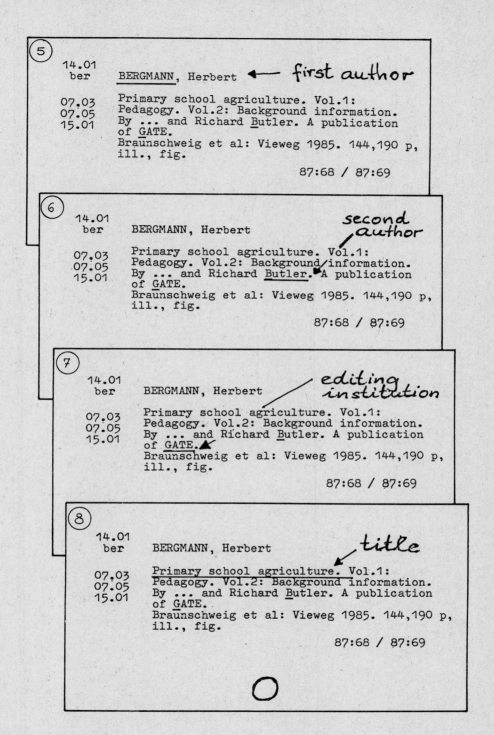

5

14.01
ber

BERGMANN, Herbert ← *first author*

07.03
07.05
15.01

Primary school agriculture. Vol.1:
Pedagogy. Vol.2: Background information.
By ... and Richard Butler. A publication
of GATE.
Braunschweig et al: Vieweg 1985. 144,190 p,
ill., fig.

87:68 / 87:69

6

14.01
ber

BERGMANN, Herbert

second author

07.03
07.05
15.01

Primary school agriculture. Vol.1:
Pedagogy. Vol.2: Background information.
By ... and Richard Butler. A publication
of GATE.
Braunschweig et al: Vieweg 1985. 144,190 p,
ill., fig.

87:68 / 87:69

7

14.01
ber

BERGMANN, Herbert

editing institution

07.03
07.05
15.01

Primary school agriculture. Vol.1:
Pedagogy. Vol.2: Background information.
By ... and Richard Butler. A publication
of GATE.
Braunschweig et al: Vieweg 1985. 144,190 p,
ill., fig.

87:68 / 87:69

8

14.01
ber

BERGMANN, Herbert

title

07.03
07.05
15.01

Primary school agriculture. Vol.1:
Pedagogy. Vol.2: Background information.
By ... and Richard Butler. A publication
of GATE.
Braunschweig et al: Vieweg 1985. 144,190 p,
ill., fig.

87:68 / 87:69

Fig. 52 continued

11. Physical Processing of Books/Documents

Books and other library materials must be physically prepared for the shelves and for circulation. Marks of ownership, lettering and other spine markings and special binding for unbound materials are required.

11.1 Ownership Marks

As already described in Chapter 2, all books and documents should be stamped with the library stamp in order to identify ownership. The call number and the accession number should also be recorded adjacent to the stamp. The accession number is entered into the book after it has been registered in the accessions book; the call number will be entered after the book has been classified.

11.2 Call Number

A call number is a number assigned to a book to distinguish it from others and to indicate its place on the shelves. A call number is composed of two

elements: the main class number and the first three letters of the main heading (author's name or title for anonymous works).

Examples:

20.07
sas

(Biogas)
Sasse = author = main heading

12.07
urb

(Sanitation)
Urban Sanitation Planning Manual = title = main heading

The call numbers for nonbook materials are usually composed of the respective symbol and the accession number — see Chapter 9 ''Nonbook Materials'' for further information.

The call number is typed on self-adhesive labels. If you cannot buy them in an office supply shop near you, prepare you own. Take a white sheet of paper and draw horizontal and vertical lines the size of the labels (approx. 2 × 3.5 cm). Use the first sheet as a master copy, i.e. photocopy the sheet of paper several times — it will save you time. You then can type the call numbers, cut them and paste them to the spine of the book.
If a book has a dust jacket, you should either remove the jacket before labelling the book or protect the book (and the jacket) with a plastic cover so that the dust cover cannot be removed by users. Only then should the call number label be pasted to the book.

Try to label each book the same distance from the bottom, about 5 to 10 mm, so that the books look tidy on the shelves and can be more easily shelved and located. All labels should be secured with transparent tape.

call number
horizontal

If the document is too narrow to carry the call number horizontally, it can be lettered vertically. The marking should always run in the same direction, preferably in the same direction as the title.

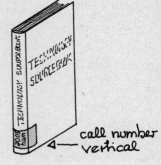

If the spine is too thin for the call number, put the label in the lower left-hand corner of the front cover. Part of the label should be visible on the spine.

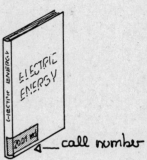

Before placing the labelled books on the shelves cross-check the call number on the spine of the book against the one on the title page!

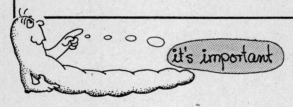

11.3 Labelling on Spine

If a book is not to be borrowed, i.e. removed from the library, add a label to that effect. This applies to all reference books (encyclopedias, directories, dictionaries, atlases, etc.) which should always be available and therefore are not to be borrowed. You may mark them with an ''R'' or ''Ref'' (for reference) on the spine just above the call number. In addition, labels with the note "FOR REFERENCE ONLY" can be prepared and put on the title page.

If you want to mark all documents relevant to your specific region or country, stick a piece of coloured tape on top of the call number. When browsing through the shelves for geographical information, the users will immediately recognize all documents of regional importance.

11.4 Binding of Documents

Unbound documents which you want to treat as a monograph, i.e. place them on the shelves, should be bound. It is quite easy to bind such documents yourself. Two pieces of cardboard the size of the document to be bound are placed at the front and the back and then stapled. A plastic or cloth tape (ca. 4 cm wide) is pasted on the spine. The colour of the tape should be white or cream in order to be able to write the author and title of the document (if necessary in an abridged form) on the spine.

131

11.5 "Spine" Title

Have you ever found yourself in the following situation? You are searching for a given document but you cannot find it on the shelves because most of the documents look the same — a black or white spine blank except for the call number. You have to take out nearly every document within a given class number, open it and look at the title page in order to find out whether it is the document you want. Unfortunately, many international and national organizations, consulting firms and government offices, i.e. most noncommercial publishers, do not print the title and author's name on the spine of the document. This is frustrating for the librarian as well as for the user. That is why we recommend marking the blank spines with the title and author information. The procedure is simple: Type the author's name (first one only, and use the acronym for organizations, if possible) and the title (if it is a long one, abridge it) on a sheet of paper, cut it to size, paste it to the spine and cover it with transparent tape. The users of your library will be most grateful for this service!

11.6 Shelving

The processed books and documents will be arranged on the shelves according to their call numbers, i.e. according to class numbers and within each class number in alphabetical order according to the author's name.

When you first start arranging the books do not overcrowd the shelves as (1) books suffer damage when they are forced in and out of spaces too small for them and (2) you will not have any space for new additions . **It is best to fill each shelf only half or three-quarters full so that new books can be easily added.** And it is also advisable to leave the bottom shelf free for further expansion. At first sight, this seems to be a waste of valuable shelf space but you will soon realize that it prevents you from constantly having to shift all the books in order to make room for new ones.

Each bookshelf should have an identifying label to help locate books easily and quickly. Shelf label holders are available from library supply distributors. But you can also do without them if they are hard to obtain in your country. Simply cut cardboard into pieces of approx. 1.5 cm × 12 cm (the width depends on the width of your shelves), label them with the respective class numbers, protect the writing with transparent tape and paste them to the shelves.

The labelling of shelves is best done after the books are in position. Only then will you know for which class groups labels are actually needed. If, for instance, you only have 20 documents in the entire macro-group

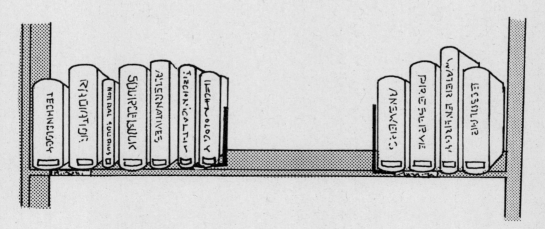

"05.00 — Politics ..." it would be pointless to label each main group separately. In such a case it is sufficient to prepare one label only for the entire group.

If books have to be shifted at some later time because there is not enough space left on a bookshelf for further additions, do not forget to move the labels too.

Advertising new additions

New additions to the library should be publicized by displaying them in a prominent place and by circulating a list of new books at regular intervals. Display shelves are available ready made or can be made to order by your local carpenter.

12. Acquisition

Acquisition is the basis of all documentation services; it ensures that the materials for which there is a predictable demand are in the collection. Most documentation centres for which this manual is intended are special libraries as they specialize in one or several subjects. The specialization depends on the nature and scope of the parent organization. Therefore, any sensible acquisition policy must be laid down in cooperation with the staff members and the users and in accordance with the activities of the parent organization. The selection, i.e. the decision as to which books to keep (in case of donations) and which books to acquire, should never be made by the librarian alone. That is beyond the scope of a librarian's duties. It is best to establish a library committee which is also responsible for selecting new books. But the librarian should be a member of this committee and should be able to suggest titles.

12.1 Acquisition Policy

The acquisition policy of an organization depends on a number of factors:

(1) **Budget.** The organization should allocate a certain amount of money for the purchase of books and periodicals in its annual budget. There is also the possibility that donor agencies give grants for the purchase of foreign books.

(2) **Objectives and priorities of the parent organization.** In which field is the library supposed to specialize? Not everything can or should be acquired.

(3) **Type of user, users' needs**. Do the users require scientific materials or simple, practical information?

(4) **Relationship with other libraries and documentation centres.** Are there any libraries in your area from which you could borrow books seldom needed in your library, i.e. to which you could refer the users?

(5) **Specialty.** Is there an agreement between your organization and others (nationally or internationally) on which fields your library is supposed to specialize in and which other libraries exist to exchange information with? Since libraries all over the world tend to have limited budgets, such agreements are recommended. Library A, for instance, collects all documents on textile finishing including natural dyes, weaving techniques, etc., Library B specializes in biogas technology, and Library C in organic farming techniques. Thus, each member of such an information network has access to a wider range of information than it could possibly collect on its own.

(6) **Library staff.** The number of new acquisitions depends also on the number of library staff and their capacity. It is pointless to acquire a lot of new books if the staff are not capable of processing them.

(7) **Languages.** A decision is needed regarding the major language of the collection as well as foreign language materials (which ones, to what extent?).

Acquisition policy is not only related to the books you have to pay for but also to those which you are offered free of charge. It often happens that individuals or organizations donate books to libraries. Sometimes people want to dispose of books they no longer need but they do not want to throw them away. Therefore, they donate them to a library. As long as the subject of the books fits into your collection you should, of course, accept them. But be careful not to accept old editions or books not related to your specialized field. Novels or children's books, for instance, are of no use in your specialized collection. And if, for instance, you are specializing in agriculture, a student's textbook on medicine would be out of place in your library! You will be busy enough processing those documents you have ordered, so be restrictive in accepting donations. The same applies to foreign language books. It does not make sense to keep books nobody will ever read. Do not waste time and space cataloguing such materials.

As already mentioned in Chapter 1, part of the acquisition policy is **weeding. Once a year, preferably at the same time as stocktaking, you should weed the collection,** i.e. discard all books irrelevant to the purposes of the library. Such books include: (a) old editions of textbooks if a more recent one is available; (b) out-of-date directories and yearbooks when a current edition has been received; (c) damaged and worn books and documents — if they are of continued value in your library, order a new copy. Discard the superseded books only after having received and processed replacement copies.

If you do not want to throw away the books you have sorted out, offer them to your colleagues and/or users and/or other libraries.

12.2 Tracing and Selection of Books and Documents

Documents on specific subjects can be traced through the following information sources:

— special bibliographies
— bibliographies contained in primary documents
— subject specialists
— publishers' catalogues
— national and international organizations and
— other libraries (catalogues and acquisition lists).

The best sources of information about **new publications** are publishers' catalogues, acquisition lists from other libraries, and book reviews in periodicals.

The staff members to whom a periodical is regularly circulated should be asked to read the book reviews and announcements and mark the ones of potential importance to the library.

The librarian, too, should regularly and thoroughly scan periodicals, publishers' catalogues, and library acquisition lists for publications of possible use to the library and compile a list of these proposals for the library committee. Book reviews and announcements of new publications in periodicals are an important source of information. Check to see if the book in question is distributed free of charge to institutions in developing countries. Some international and national development organizations have adopted this practice as part of their information policy.

On the basis of the list of books suggested for acquisition compiled by the librarian, the **library committee** decides whether a particular item should be ordered. Before submitting the list, the librarian should check each item against the author catalogue and the orders file to ensure that the book is not already in the collection or on order. Apart from the general acquisition policy the library committee should also base its decision on the following questions:

— Does the book actually fill a gap in the collection or is the subject already well covered?
— Is the information more up to date, more comprehensive, or more helpfully presented than in any other documents held?
— How often will it be consulted?
— How expensive is it (including postage)? Are there any restrictions regarding foreign exchange acquisitions?

12.3 Ordering Procedure

There are two ways of acquiring documents: by paying for them or by obtaining them free of charge.

Documents you have to pay for can either be ordered at a local bookshop or directly from the publisher. Before placing orders for foreign books with any local bookshop, make sure that they can handle foreign orders. In many countries there are bookshops specializing in handling foreign books. Books however can also be ordered directly from the publisher although some publishers are reluctant to supply single copies to individuals abroad. In order to save postage and to receive books faster, it is advisable to ask colleagues travelling abroad to buy books and bring them back.

Once you have decided where to order the books, the appropriate addresses have to be located. For quick and easy reference, it is useful to build up an address file of bookshops, publishers and organizations.

Each order is typed on an **order letter** stating order number, author, title, edition, publisher, date of publication, and number of copies required for each item listed. If the bibliographic information is incomplete, it can be helpful to add the source of information. You should also mention whether the books are to be sent by sea or air mail. If known, the ISBN[1] and ISSN[2] should also be stated. You may use a standard order letter (see sample form letters at the end of this chapter).

[1] ISBN = International Standard Book Number
[2] ISSN = International Standard Serials Number.

A copy of the order letter is kept in the orders file and arranged in alphabetical order according to the supplier's name. Every three to six months, the orders file is checked and reminders are sent. (Checking is easier when the orders are filed by item ordered; but then you have to type a separate order for each item.)

When parcels of books arrive, the contents are checked against the invoice. The librarian initials the invoice to acknowledge its correctness and passes it on to the Accounts Department for payment. The books are then entered in the accessions book and further processed as described above.

Restrictions on foreign exchange can be overcome by purchasing UNESCO international coupons or SATIS tokens. **UNESCO international coupons** can be obtained from your national UNESCO office and are paid for in your national currency. All UN organizations (such as FAO, UNIDO, UNEP and, of course, the UN sales offices and UNESCO itself) and quite a number of commercial publishers accept these coupons as payment.

SATIS tokens are available from the SATIS Secretariat and are sold in units of US$ 25. SATIS tokens are only accepted by SATIS member bookshops. For more information see the SATIS catalogue which can be obtained from the SATIS Secretariat. (Address: SATIS Secretariat, P.O. Box 803, NL-3500 AV Utrecht, Netherlands).

To obtain information about **unpublished documents, generally distributed free of charge,** is usually more difficult than to actually acquire the documents themselves. You can only find out about so-called unpublished documents (reports, studies, evaluation reports, conference papers, etc.) by checking bibliographies, through personal contact with authors and organizations or by examining catalogues of national and international organizations and government agencies. Once you have traced these documents, you should write to the publishing institution and ask for a copy. It is advisable to include some information about your own organization and a brief explanation of why you need the document. A copy of the letter should be kept in the orders file. Books and documents that can be obtained free of charge should be ordered in the same way as other book materials. See form letter at the end of this chapter.

12.4 Acquiring/Ordering Periodicals

The number of periodicals published each year is immense and it is difficult to identify those actually needed by a small organization. You will, of
course, need those published in your country in your specialized field
and/or newsletters from organizations you work with. Ask established
AT documentation centres for recommendations about periodicals
published worldwide on appropriate technology, rural development,
renewable energy resources and agriculture.

Many periodicals are distributed free of charge. In such cases, you should
simply ask the publisher to be put on the mailing list. But be restrictive in
subscribing to them even if they are free of charge, because periodicals are
time-consuming to deal with. Be equally restrictive in subscribing to
periodicals you have to pay for because they usually are quite expensive.
Before ordering any periodical, it is advisable to obtain a sample copy
from the publisher. You will then have full and accurate publication details and can judge for yourself whether it is relevant to your library collection.

Each order should be typed in duplicate: one copy is sent to the publisher
and one copy is retained for the orders file. They are filed in a separate
section of the orders file in alphabetical order according to the title of the
periodical. The order should contain the title of the periodical, ISSN (if
known), publisher, frequency, price, and number and volume the order
starts with. Remember that periodicals often have to be prepaid.

When the periodicals arrive you should proceed as described in Chapter
9.1.

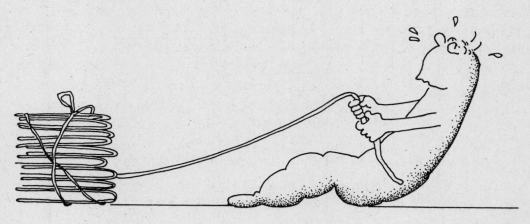

```
             Letter head of your organization
                         LIBRARY


                     ACCESSIONS LIST
             Period: January - March 1987


02.00    DEVELOPMENT, INTERNATIONAL COOPERATION

Ghai, Dharam / Martin Godfrey / Franklin Lisk: Planning for basic
     needs in Kenya. Performance, policies and prospects. 2nd
     impr. Geneva:ILO 1980. (02.02)

International Development Research Centre (IDRC): Projects 1970-
     1981. Ottawa:IDRC 1982. 384 p  (02.06.01/int)

Central Building Research Institute Roorkee: Annual report
     1985-86. Roorkee 1986. 136 p    (02.06.03/cen)
etc



10.00 SCIENCE, RESEARCH AND TECHNOLOGY


deMoll, Lane (Ed.): Rainbook. Resources for appropriate techno-
     logy. New York: Schocken 1977. 250 p.  (10.03/dem)

Environmental and Development Agency (EDA): People's workbook.
  Working together to change your community. Johannesburg 1981.
     560 p   (10.03/env)

Thorburn, Craig: Teknologi kampungan. A collection of indigenous
     Indonesian technologies. Stanford, Calif.: Volunteers in Asia
     1982. 154 p   (10.03/tho)

etc



19.00    INDUSTRY AND MANUFACTURE, SERVICES


Vogler, Jan: Small scale recycling of plastics. London: IT Publ.
     1984. 94 p   (19.05/vog)

Norsker, Hendrik: The self-reliant potter: Refractories and
  kilns. A GATE publication. Braunschweig: Viewe 1987. 134 p
     (19.13/nor)
```

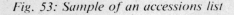

Fig. 53: Sample of an accessions list

12.5 Accessions List

To inform users about newly acquired books, an accessions list should be prepared every three months. The accessions list is best compiled by main classification group and within each group in alphabetical order according to author. The easiest way to compile the accessions list probably is to keep the catalogue cards for the classified catalogue and to only file them after the accessions list has been typed. But if you are using a card duplicator for the reproduction of catalogue cards, you can also prepare one more card to be used for the accessions list. The number of distribution copies required will influence your decision on how to duplicate the accessions list. If it is meant for internal use only, photocopying is sufficient. But if you intend to send it to external users and other organizations, the use of a stencil machine is recommended in order to save on duplicating costs.
A suggested form for an accessions list is given in Fig. 53.

12.6 Form Letters

1. Ordering books and documents you have to pay for

```
Re: Order No. 88/6                  date ...

Dear Sir / Madam,
We hereby order the book(s) listed below / in the enclosed
list:
. . . . . . . . . . . . . . .
. . . . . . . . . . . . . . .
We would be grateful if you could send them by sea mail /
by air mail to our above / below address.
Please bill us.


Yours faithfully
Librarian
```

2. Reminder

```
Re: Our order number ... dated ...

Dear Sir / Madam,
We have checked our records and find that the book(s)
listed below have not yet arrived.
...............
...............
We would be grateful if you could inform us wether the books
were dispatched by you (if so, when) and wether they are
still available.
Yours fathfully
Librarian
```

3. Ordering free publications

```
                                        date ...
Re: Request for books - our order number: ...

Dear Sir / Madam,
We would be very grateful if you could supply us with the
following books. We learned from a note in .............
(here follows the title of the periodical, vol., no., date)
that you distribute them free of charge to organizations
in developing countries.
...................
...................

Thanking you very much in advance, we remain
Yours faithfully
Librarian
```

13. Dissemination of Information (Loan Policy)

While reading the manual so far, haven't you sometimes asked yourself whether the work involved in setting up a documentation centre is worth the trouble? Why take the trouble not just to collect information but also to process it? The answer is simple. **The ultimate purpose of a documentation centre or a library is to disseminate information.** The very existence of a documentation centre is only justified by making maximum use of its collection. A library that serves as a mere repository of books does not deserve its name. To merely collect books should never be an end in itself. If not used as extensively as possible by its users, a library is futile. And maximum use of a collection can only be made if the books are properly processed and if the library pursues a dynamic dissemination policy.

A dynamic dissemination policy does not exclude the risk of losses. There is not a library in the world, especially those maintaining an open-shelf collection, where books do not go missing from time to time. The only way to exclude losses would be to keep the collection permanently under lock and key which would be self-defeating. One or other of the readers will now object "Isn't it better to lock the books away than to have them

145

stolen? We cannot afford to constantly replace lost books." There is some truth in this, particularly if expensive books are lost. But it is still better that a book be stolen and thus, one can presume, be read and used than safely locked away and never read. In order to avoid any misunderstanding: this is not an invitation for people to steal books and it is not a justification of theft. But it should be made clear that dissemination of information is never possible without risking losses.

When cataloguing and classifying, filing and shelving always bear in mind that the user is the focal point of all information systems. **It is the user and his/her needs on which your activities should be focused.** But quite often users do not know which services they can expect from a documentation centre. So it is up to you to inform them about the various services and materials available and attract them to the library. In industry this is called marketing. And just as no commercial enterprise can survive without a dynamic marketing strategy, in the long term no documentation centre can do without a dynamic dissemination policy.

13.1 Basic Principles for the Dissemination of Information

Some basic marketing principles should be applied in your information dissemination process:

(1) **Know your users and their needs and provide and disseminate information accordingly.** This involves talking to the users, knowing what they are presently working on, and knowing their fields of interest. Only then can you advise them well and refer them to new and interesting publications that they may not have asked for and that perhaps they were not even aware of. On the other hand, the user may give you valuable advice on the existence and quality of new publications. A good relationship between the librarian and the user benefits both.

(2) **The library should be organized in such a way that it invites the readers to browse through the collection.** The layout of the library should be logical, the labelling of the shelves should be clearly recognizable, the classification scheme should be prominently displayed (in transparent folders, if available), and there should be a work area for the use of the

146

readers — in a word: the atmosphere should be inviting. On entering the library, the user should have the feeling of being welcomed, of not being an intruder. Remember that many people are afraid of entering a library. This is particularly true in rural areas. The librarian should help them to overcome the fear of entering a strange place. You can do so by giving each newcomer a brief personal introduction and/or by preparing a leaflet explaining the system applied and the services offered, i.e. how to use a catalogue, how to find a subject in the classification scheme, how to make best use of the various files, etc. The loan policy should be flexible, not restrictive.

(3) **Provide good reference services.** Keep your collection up to date. Make sure that books often required are actually available, i.e. reference books, maps, basic handbooks, etc., should not be borrowed. Books frequently required are to be lent out for a short period only and/or a second copy should be provided. An accessions list should be prepared at regular intervals (preferably quarterly) to inform the users about new books acquired by the library. The opening hours should be regular and as long as possible. During those hours the library should not be left unattended in case a user needs your help. You are the one who knows best what is available in the library as you are the one who catalogued and classified the books. Do not expect the newcomer to already know how to make best use of the library. **But do not be exploited by the user — it is the user who has to do the research and not the librarian.** Specific requests for data (addresses, figures, etc.) can be answered; however, extensive research involving the checking of many publications for information requiring interpretation and evaluation is not your task. Your task is to inform users in which books information required by them is most likely to be found and where the book has been placed.

13.2 Loan Procedures

Each library should decide beforehand on certain loan procedures:

(a) **Who is entitled to borrow books?** Only staff members of the organization or external users as well? It is advisable to allow free access to the library to everybody without restrictions.

(b) How many books may be borrowed? Not more than five books per person at a time should be lent out. Exceptions should be permitted, however.

(c) Which books may be borrowed? There should be some restrictions regarding the loan of reference books, frequently required handbooks, periodicals, pamphlets, clippings, maps and atlases. These materials are for in-library use only. (That is why you need a working place for the readers.)

(d) How long are books to be lent out? The normal period should be four weeks. Renewal for another two to four weeks should be possible if the books are not required by another reader.

(e) Opening hours. The library should be open during working hours, depending on the customs in your country. But the library should not be left unattended as (a) the risk of losses thus increases and (b) the users may need your help.

(f) Loan slips. It is obvious that some kind of record is needed in order to be able to ascertain who has borrowed books and when these are to be returned. This can either be done with book cards or loan slips. Since the preparation of book cards involves a considerable amount of additional work, we suggest a loan slip system. The additional work is done by the user and not by the librarian. The library provides the forms which are to be completed at the time of lending by the user (see sample at the end of this chapter). The loan slip is filed in numerical order according to the call number. The loan slips should be the same size as the catalogue cards and are kept in open card trays.

The following information should be recorded on a loan slip:

— identity of the book (call number, author, title, and accession number if the publication consists of several volumes or copies)
— identity of the borrower (name, address, telephone number)
— date of the loan.

The loan slips are reviewed regularly once a month. When a loan period expires, reminders are sent to borrowers (see sample at the end of this chapter). If the books are not returned after several reminders, the books can be regarded as lost and the borrower becomes liable for the cost of replacement. Therefore the librarian, should always be informed before a staff member leaves the organization in order to recall books still out on loan or to demand payment of the cost of replacement.

Sample form of a loan slip:

```
Call no.: .......        Date: .............

Author: ............................................

Title: .............................................

....................................................

Accession no.: .....................................

Name of borrower: ..................................

Address: ...........................................
```

Form letter/postcard for overdue books:

```
To:
From:  Librarian
Subject: Overdue books          Date: ...........


The following books have been on loan to you since ...
We would be grateful if you could either return them
or renew them as soon as possible.

1. (Author/Title/Call no.) ..........................
2. ..................................................
3. ..................................................
4. ..................................................
```

13.3 Circulation of Periodicals

Current issues of periodicals should not be lent out to external users. The staff members of the organization, i.e. the internal users, should be given priority access to periodicals which have newly arrived.

There are various possibilities for an **effective periodical usage policy:**

(1) All new periodicals are displayed in the library for about one to two weeks so that all users can be informed equally. If somebody is interested in a particular article he may read it in the library or ask for a photocopy.

(2) New periodicals are circulated among the staff members of the organization. This is a widespread practice in many organizations' libraries, but apart from the advantage of supplying readers with unsolicited information, there are some disadvantages:

(a) It sometimes takes too long for the last one on the circulation list gets the periodical.

(b) There may be some staff members who are not always in the office and therefore keep it for long periods, thereby causing delays.

(c) Periodicals may become damaged or lost while circulating.

(d) It is difficult to trace a particular issue when it is requested by somebody else.

(e) It may be difficult to establish a priority list of who should be the first to see various periodicals.

(3) Probably the most effective way to disseminate information in journals equally to all staff members and users and to solve the above-mentioned problems is to circulate photocopies of the title page and the list of contents. Users are thus kept informed and can come to the library to read or photocopy articles of interest.

14. Layout, Furniture and Equipment

Before making any decision on the layout and installation of a documentation centre, it is essential to identify the actual needs of the centre, i.e. the expected size of the collection, and the primary users.

It is advisable to have a separate room for the library which is large enough to allow further expansion. A 10% increase per year should be calculated. When the library is established, shelf capacity should be sufficient for at least three years. In concrete terms, if you start with approximately 1,500 volumes, the collection will have grown to approx. 2.000 volumes within three years . Generally, a 1-m shelf will hold 50 books/documents; but as the shelves should only be filled three quarters full you will need ca. 50 m shelving for 2,000 titles.

14.1 Layout

The actual layout of the library depends on the space and the budget provided by the organization. A few general considerations should however always be taken into account.

Even if the documentation centre occupies a single room (we assume that this is the case for most libraries using this manual), the different work areas should be clearly laid out.

When the library is managed by only one person, the **work post of the librarian** should be in a strategic place where users can be seen coming in and out. Besides a desk and chair, the librarian's work station should have one or two filing cabinets for supplies, stationary, the storage of books and documents being processed, correspondence and order files; an additional table for the handling of documents; a typewriter; a telephone; and necessary stationary for daily clerical tasks, including library supplies such as record cards for periodicals and trays for loan slips.

The area for the collection or stacks should be large enough to allow easy access to the shelves. The distance between shelves should not be less than 70 cm; preferred distance is 90 cm. Library furniture should be specially designed for library use and purchased locally — either ready made or made to order by local craftsmen. Make sure to buy good quality as the shelves will be used for many years.

The catalogue cabinet should be placed near the shelves.

The readers' area should consist of a medium-sized table and four chairs. The library should be well lit.

Atmospheric conditions must also be taken into account while planning the layout of a library. Excessive humidity and excessive draught are equally harmful. Air conditioning is probably the best solution for tropical countries but it is very expensive if used continuously. Natural cross-ventilation and a fan/ventilator will help to reduce the heat. Make sure that the windows can be opened. Shelves should never be placed directly in front of windows. It is also advisable not to use the sunniest room of the office for the library, as overexposure to sun damages books.

On the following page, additional suggestions for the layout of a small documentation centre are given.

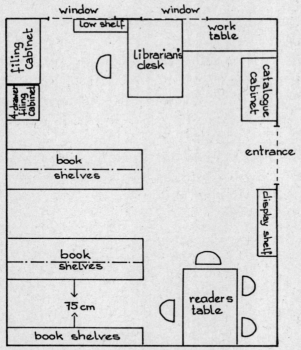

Library room, shelving space: 50 m ≈ 2.000 volumes

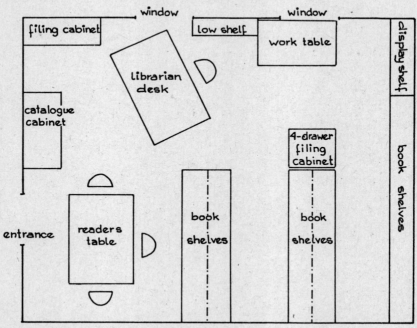

Library room 20 m² (4 × 5 m)
shelving space: 55 m ≈ 2.200 volumes

154

14.2 List of Furniture and Equipment Needed

The items listed below are indispensable for all libraries. Standard library furniture is available from library furniture suppliers. Ask your nearest public library for information. To gain an impression of what the items listed below look like, request a catalogue from a library supplier even if you are not going to order right away.

Maintain a three-month supply of stationary, particularly when supplies are difficult to obtain.

Furniture

— shelves (25 m per 1000 volumes)
1 desk (librarian)
1 chair (librarian)
1 work table (librarian)
1 table (users)
4 chairs (users)
1–2 filing cabinets (metal or wood) which can be locked
1 filing cabinet with 4 drawers (metal)
1 catalogue cabinet and stand (minimum: 5 drawers)
1 display shelf for periodicals and/or new books (optional)

Equipment and stationery

1 ' typewriter
1   photocopier, or access to a photocopier
1   telephone
1   duplicator (incl. stencils, ink, etc.)
—   bookends (ca. 40 per 1000 volumes)
2   open trays for loan slips
    (dimensions: H: 8 cm × W: 17 cm × D: 25 cm)
1   open tray for record cards
    (dimensions: H: 10 cm × W: 24 cm × D: 25 cm)
—   catalogue cards (minimum of 5000 cards per 1000 volumes)
—   guide cards/catalogue dividers
—   vertical files (30 per drawer)
—   pamphlet files
—   magazine boxes made of cardboard, wood or plastic
—   loose-leaf binders
—   transparent folders
—   accessions book for books and documents
—   accessions book for nonbook materials
—   record cards for periodicals
—   rubber stamps (ownership, accession stamp)
—   white self-adhesive labels for call numbers
—   coloured labels for special markings
—   transparent tape
—   shelf labels
—   shelf label holders
—   paper punch (1 small, 1 large)
—   stapler (1 small, 1 large)
—   scissors
—   stationary (paper, pens, envelopes)

14.3 Shelves

Library shelves are usually made of wood or metal or a combinatin of both. They should be strong and of good quality. Shelves should be neither too high nor too low. If they are too high, shorter persons will have difficulty reaching the top shelf; if they are too low, you lose valuable space. It is not absolutely necessary to have adjustable shelves once you have decided on a suitable distance between shelves. Many libraries shelve taller books and pamphlet files separately, on the bottom shelf, for example, in order to save space. But in the interest of the users and in view of our aim to place all relevant materials (irrespective of size) together, a fairly large distance (38 cm) is recommended although it results in a loss of space (see also Chapter 11.6 "Shelving").

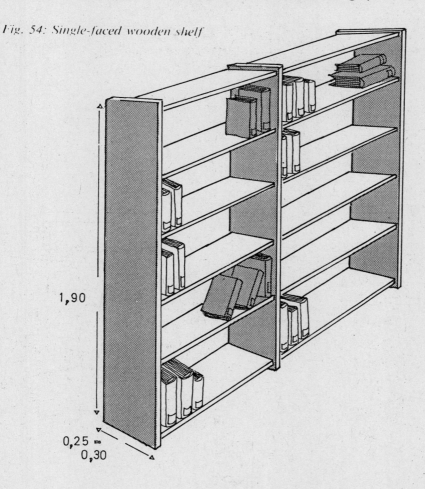

Fig. 54: Single-faced wooden shelf

1,90

0,25 –
0,30

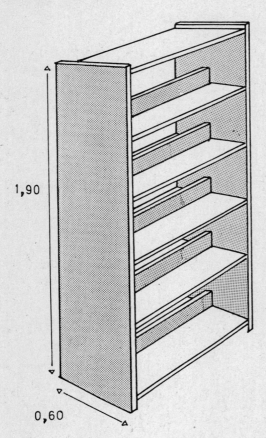

Fig. 55: Double-faced wooden shelf

1,90

0,60

Suggested dimensions of shelves:

Height: 190 cm
Width: 100 cm
Depth: 25−30 cm
Distance between shelves: 38 cm

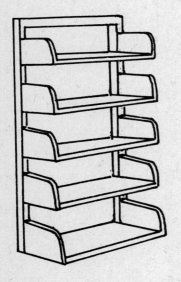

Fig. 56: Single-faced metal shelf

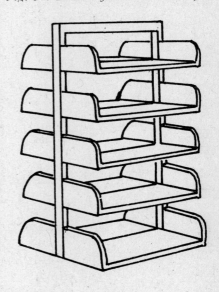

Fig. 57: Double-faced metal shelf

158

It depends on the size of the library room and the location of the windows whether the walls can be lined with single-faced shelves or whether you should use double faced shelves. Probably a combination of both is best.

14.4 Catalogue Cabinet

Card catalogue cabinets are usually made of wood. The drawers should be neither too long nor too short, and the optimal depth is 44 cm. The drawers should move easily and be equipped with a rod to hold the cards in place, a rod lock, a handle, and a window for labels. All metal parts should be of stainless steel. For estimating the size of the catalogue cabinet see Chapter 7.6 "Catalogue Maintenance".

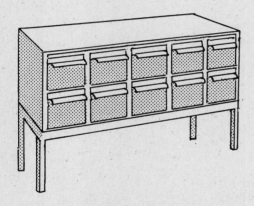

Fig. 58: Catalogue cabinet

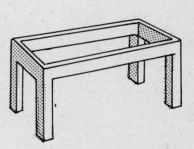

Fig. 60: Leg base or stand for catalogue cabinet

Fig. 59: Drawer for catalogue cabinet

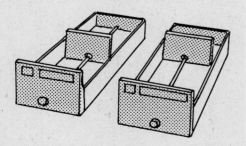

Dimensions of a drawer:

	Inside:	Outside:
Depth:	40 cm	44 cm
Height:	10 cm	18 cm
Width:	15,2 cm	19 cm

159

14.5 Duplicator

As already mentioned in Chapter 10.1 a manually operated duplicator is best for reproducing of catalogue cards in a small library. To our knowledge, the Gaylord duplicator is unique; it is durable, easy to operate, does not need electricity and is inexpensive. The starter set which includes the duplicator itself, black ink, and 100 stencils costs US$ 248.00 (as at June 1988). For ordering information, see the address at the end of this chapter.

The stencils can also be produced locally. You simply have to have the frames cut to size by your local print shop; customary stencils are available in stationary shops all over the world. You can cut one such stencil into six card catalogue stencils.

Once machine is inked, simply place stencil in carrier and slip card or pocket into holder slot in cover. Close cover.

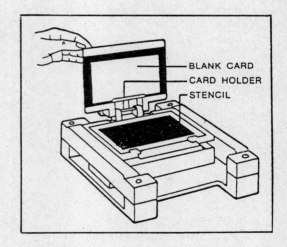

To print, just pull forward, press down and push back. Release tension, open cover and remove your printed card.

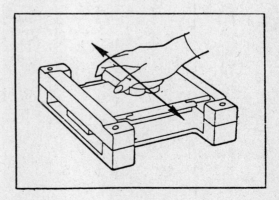

Fig. 61: Gaylord Duplicator

160

14.6 Other Equiment and Stationery (Drawings)

Fig. 62: Tray for loan slips (for approx. 600 loan slips):
Width: 17 cm
Height: 18 cm
Depth: 25 cm

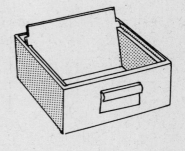

Fig. 63: Tray for record cards
(for approx. 600 cards)

Width: 25.5 cm
Height: 19 cm
Depth: 25 cm

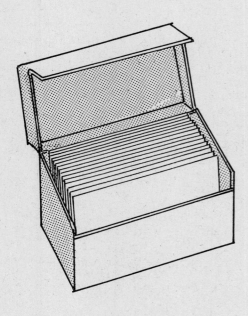

Fig. 64: Microfiche/computer disk box

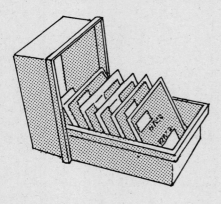

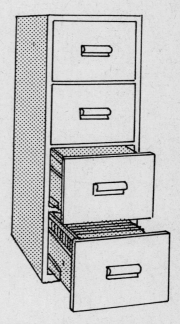

Fig. 65: Vertical file cabinet (4 drawers)

14.7 Addresses of Library Suppliers

1. Brodart
   P.O. Box 3037
   1609 Memorial Avenue
   Williamsport, PA 17705
   USA

2. DEMCO
   Box 7488
   Madison, WI 53707
   USA

3. Gaylord Bros., Inc.
   Box 4901
   Syracuse, NY 13221-4901
   USA

4. Libraco Ltd.
   Lombard Wall
   Woolwich Road
   London SE7 7RJ
   United Kingdom

5. Don Gresswell Ltd.
   Bridge House
   Grange Park
   London N21 1RB
   United Kingdom

Glossary[1]

AACR. The Anglo-American Cataloging Rules.

Accession number. A number assigned to each book as it is received in the library, for instance 88:102.

Accessions book. The book in which all books and documents are entered immediately after receipt. Nonbook materials are entered in the accessions book for nonbook materials.

Acquisition policy. The policy pursued in obtaining new materials for a collection.

Acronym. A pronounceable abbreviation/word formed by combining initial letters or syllables and letters of a series of words or a compound term.

Added entry. A secondary entry, i.e. one other than the main entry, for instance for second author, title, series, or second or third class number.

Anonymous work. A book or document in which the name of the author does not appear anywhere in the book.

Author. The person or corporate body responsible for the content of a publication — writer of a book, compiler of a bibliography, artist, photographer, etc.

Author catalogue. A card catalogue of author entries, arranged alphabetically, usually including added entries under editors, second and third authors, etc., and entries under titles in the case of anonymous works.

Bibliography. A list of books, periodical articles, or other works.

Call number. The notation used to identify and locate a particular book on the shelves. It consists of the classification number and the first three letters of the author's name.

Card catalogue. A catalogue whose entries are prepared on standard cards and filed in drawers.

---

[1] This glossary is mainly based on the glossaries prepared by B.S. Wynar and E. Piercy, respectively.

Catalogue. A list of books, maps, journals, recordings or any other medium that comprises a collection. It may be arranged by alphabet, by number, or by subject.

Cataloguing. Description of a work by its essential characteristics or bibliographic description.

Charging. The process of recording the loan of a book or other library item borrowed for use.

Class. Class number. A subject group; a subject number assigned to an item.

Classification. See classification system and classifying.

Classification schedule. The printed scheme of a particular classification system.

Classification system. A system for the arrangement of books usually according to subjects using numbers, letters, symbols or a combination of the three.

Classified catalogue. A catalogue arranged by subject (by class number) according to some classification scheme.

Classifying. Description of a work by subject (see also indexing).

Collation. Physical description of a book. It consists of the number of pages, presence of illustrations (maps, tables, graphs, charts, figures), bibliography, and appendices.

Collection. A group of books or other materials; also used for the library's entire holdings.

Compiler. One who brings together written or printed matter from the works of various authors or the works of a single author, for instance the compiler of a bibliography.

Compound name. A name formed from two or more proper names which are usually connected by a hyphen, a conjunction, or a preposition.

Copyright. The exclusive right to publish a work for a specified number of years.

Corporate author. An organization or an institution acting as the author/editor of a publication.

Cross-reference. A referral from words or names not used to the forms used in a catalogue. "See" reference and "see also" reference.

Descriptor. Clearly defined term of a thesaurus or any list of controlled vocabulary used as subject heading.

Dust jacket. The paper cover laid around a book.

Edition. A distinctive text of a published work; each new edition implies additions to, or other changes in, the text.

Editor. One who prepares for publication or supervises the publication of a work or collection of works that is not his/her own.

Entry. A record of a bibliographic entity in a catalogue.

Entry word. Usually the first word of the heading by which the entry is arranged in the catalogue. (Author's name, or first word of the title other than an article.)

Format. The physical make-up of a work: size, binding, printing, etc.

Guide card. A card slightly higher than the catalogue cards, carrying letters, names or words indicating the material directly behind it in the catalogue. It is inserted in a card catalogue to help the user find a desired place of heading in the catalogue.

Heading. Any word, name or phrase placed at the head of a catalogue card to indicate some special aspect of the book.

Imprint. The place, the name of the publisher, and the date of publication on the catalogue card (in that order).

Indexing. The art of identifying the subjects contained in a given publication and matching these identified subjects with the corresponding terms listed in pre-established lists of subject headings or thesauri.

International Standard Book Number (ISBN). A code number assigned by a publisher to a specific book or edition of a book.

International Standard Serial Number (ISSN). A distinctive number assigned to serials (periodicals).

Joint author. A person partially responsible for the content of a publication.

Main entry card. A full catalogue entry which gives all the information necessary for the complete identification of a work.

Monograph. A complete bibliographic unit. It may be a single work or a collection that is not a serial.

Nonbook materials. Several types of special materials. Among nonbook materials are maps, pamphlets, periodicals, motion pictures, microforms, photographs, slides, sound recordings, and video tapes.

Open entry. A part of the descriptive cataloguing not completed at the time of cataloguing. Used for incomplete works such as serials, series, etc.

Periodical. A publication with a distinctive title intended to appear in successive (usually unbound) numbers or parts at stated or regular intervals and, as a rule, for an indefinite period.

Pseudonym. Fictitious or assumed name used by an author to conceal his/her identity.

Publication date. The year a publication appears.

Publisher. The person, corporate body, or firm responsible for issuing printed matter.

Publisher's catalogue. A listing by a publisher of his/her current publications and publications in print.

Reference book. (1) A book, such as an encyclopedia or dictionary, used to obtain specific information quickly. (2) A book restricted to use within the library.

"See" reference. A referral from a heading not used to a heading used.

"See also" reference. A reference indicating related entries or headings.

Serial. A publication issued in successive parts and intended to be continued indefinitely (includes yearbooks, periodicals, newspapers, etc.).

Series. A number of separate works, usually related in subject or form, that are issued successively. They are usually issued by the same publisher and in uniform style, with a collective title that may appear on the title page or on the cover.

Shelf list. A record of books in a library arranged in the order in which they stand on the shelves. The main entries of the classified catalogue can also be used as shelf list.

Spine. The back of a book connecting the two covers, on which the title and author of the work usually appear.

Subject cataloguing. The assignment of class numbers and subject headings to the items of a library collection (see also: indexing).

Subject entry. The catalogue entry for a work under the subject heading.

Subject heading. A word or group of words describing the subject of a work. The process of assigning subject headings.

Subtitle. A secondary title, often used to expand or to limit the title proper.

Thesaurus. A collection of descriptors — generally within a special field of knowledge — which not only lists the terms in alphabetical order but also displays their relationship. Similar to lists of subject headings.

Title. The name of a work.

Title entry. The catalogue record of a work under the title. It may be a main entry or an added entry.

Title page. A page that occurs very near the beginning of a book and that contains the most complete bibliographic information about the book.

Tracing. The record on the main entry card of all the additional entries under which the work is listed in the catalogue.

Unit card. The basic catalogue card, in the form of the main entry, which when duplicated may be used as a unit for all other entries for that work in the catalogue by underlining/marking or typing the appropriate heading.

Vertical file. A file of large drawers in which folders containing pamphlets, pictures, clippings, maps, etc., are arranged

Work slip (or process slip). A card or piece of paper that accompanies a book throughout the cataloguing and preparation processes. The cataloguer notes on the work slip any directions and information needed to prepare catalogue entries, cross-references, etc.

References and Selected Further Readings

I. Cataloguing and Classifying

1. **Aman,** Mohammed M. (Ed.): Cataloging and classification of non-Western material: concerns, issues and practices. Oryx Press 1980. 368 p.

2. **Forget,** Jacqueline P.: Practical documentation. A training package for librarians. Module 1−10. London: International Planned Parenthood Federation 1978. sep. paging.

3. **Foubert,** Charles-Henri: The IDOC documentation handbook. A guide to appropriate technology and information systems. Rome: IDOC 1982. 97 p.

4. **Guinchat,** Claire and Michel **Menou**: General introduction to the techniques of information and documentation work. Paris: UNESCO 1983. 340 p.

5. **Hoffman,** Herbert H.: Small library cataloging. Santa Ana, Calif: Headway 1977. 213 p.

6. **Lendvay,** Olga: Primer for agricultural libraries. 2nd edition revised and enlarged. Wageningen: Centre for Agric. Publ. and Documentation 1980. 91 p.

7. **Morin-Labatut,** Gisèle and Maureen **Sly**: Manual for the preparation of records in development-information systems. Ottawa: IDRC 1982 (IDRC-TS40e). (Recommended methods for development-information systems. Vol. 1.)

8. **Piercy,** Esther J.: Commonsense cataloging. A manual for the organization of books and other materials in school and small public libraries. 2nd ed. revised by Marian Sanner. New York: Wilson 1974. 233 p.

9. **Wynar,** Bohdan S.: Introduction to cataloging and classification. 5th edition. Littleton, Colo.: Libraries Unltd 1976. 426 p.

II. Classification Schedules and Thesauri

1. **Dewey Decimal Classification** and Relative Index. 11th abridged edition. New York: Forest Press 1979.

2. **Gesellschaft für Information und Dokumentation (GID):** Thesaurus Guide. Analytical directory of selected vocabularies for information retrieval, 1985. Prepared for the Commission of the EC. Amsterdam et al.: North Holland; Luxembourg: EC 1985. 749 p.

3. **SATIS Classification.** 2nd edition. Amsterdam: 1983. 116 p. (available in English, French and Spanish).

4. **Universal Decimal Classification.** Abridged English edition. 3rd rev. ed. London: British Standards Institution 1961. 245 p.

5. **Viet,** Jean: Macrothesaurus for information processing in the field of economic and social development. 3rd ed. New York: UN 1985. 347 p. (English, French, Spanish).

III. Information Processing by Computer

Woods, R.G. and C.M. **Phillips:** Managing library computers. Bradford: MCB Publications 1981. 46 p.

If you are interested in computerized information processing and need suitable software, write to

UNESCO Library, Archives and
Documentation Services
7, Place de Fontenoy
F-75700 PARIS/FRANCE

UNESCO provides its **CDS/ISIS** program free of charge to institutions in its member countries.

IV. Training Opportunities

Dosa, Marta L. and Jean **Collin:** Register of short-term education and training activities in librarianship, information science and archives (English, French, Spanish). 2nd ed. Paris: Fédération Internationale de Documentation (FID) 187 p. (FID publication 647).

Annex I
Rural Development Classification (RDC) Model for Small Libraries Working in the Field of Rural Development and Appropriate Technology

Contents

170

01.00 General reference

01.01 Encyclopedias, directories

01.02 Dictionaries, glossaries, language courses, terminology (all languages)

01.03 Maps, atlases (all subjects)

01.04 Bibliographies (comprising several subjects only), publishers' catalogues, acquisition lists

01.05 International statistical yearbooks (covering several subjects only)

02.00 Development, international cooperation

02.01 Development policy and theory, international cooperation

02.02 Development, national planning, national plans

02.03 Project planning and evaluation (incl. project management and dissemination strategies)

02.04 Regional development and planning incl. regional profiles
02.04.01 Rural development

02.05 Nongovernmental organizations (NGOs) in general, self-help organizations (their role in development).
For specific organizations such as women's or peasants' see respective class within 06.

02.06 Organizations, institutions
(directories, yearbooks, annual reports, etc.)
02.06.01 International organizations
02.06.02 Regional organizations
02.06.03 National organizations

03.00 Economics, economic policy

03.01 Macroeconomics, economic theory (textbooks and general works)

03.02 Economic and social situation, economic policy, country reports (incl. national statistical yearbooks)

03.03 Economic planning, economic analysis, macroeconomic planning techniques (cost-benefit analysis, etc.)

03.04 Industrial economics, industrial development, foreign investment (incl. investment policy, investment promotion) incl. multinational corporations

03.05 Finance policy (monetary and financial economics)
  03.05.01 Banking and banks
  03.05.02 Credit and credit policy

03.06 Trade and commerce

03.07 Tourism (economic and social aspects)

03.08 Labour economics
  03.08.01 Employment policy
  03.08.02 Trade unions

03.09 Cooperatives, cooperative movement
  03.09.01 Agricultural cooperatives
  03.09.02 Credit cooperatives
  03.09.03 Production cooperatives
  03.09.04 Housing cooperatives
  03.09.05 Other specific cooperatives

03.10 Consumer protection, consumers' associations

172

04.00 Business economics

04.01 Business economics (general works, textbooks)

04.02 Microeconomic planning techniques

04.03 Management and personnel management

04.04 Organization and administration, office management

04.05 Marketing

04.06 Accounting

04.07 Statistics (textbooks only)
For statistical yearbooks see respective subject.

05.00 Politics, public administration, law and legislation

05.01 Political science, politics, public administration, political theory

05.02 Foreign policy

05.03 Laws and legislation (all subjects)

05.04 Human rights, human rights violations

05.05 Defence policy, disarmament, military (incl. peace movements)

05.06 Political parties and movements

06.00 Society and culture

06.01 Social sciences, sociology
(works comprising several subgroups) incl. participatory research
and training

06.02 Society, social structure, social change, social services
06.02.01 Community development, community organizing

06.03 Social movements, social groups (e.g. minorities)

06.04 Women, feminism, women and development, women's organizations

06.05 Children and youth (youth centres)

06.06 Demography

06.07 Philosophy

06.08 History

06.09 Psychology

06.10 Anthropology, ethnology

06.11 Religion
06.11.01 Buddhism
06.11.02 Christianity incl. liberation theology, church and
development
06.11.03 Hinduism
06.11.04 Islam
06.11.05 Others

06.12 Art, folklore, music, linguistics, theatre, archeology

06.13 Sports

174

07.00 Education, training

07.01 Education and training (general works, theories, methods)

07.02 Educational facilities (schools, training centres)

07.03 Teaching methods and aids

07.04 Adult education, literacy

07.05 Primary education

07.06 Secondary education

07.07 Higher education

07.08 Vocational training
For specific training — curricula, textbooks — see specific subject.

08.00 Communication, information and documentation

08.01 Communication, telecommunication, mass communication, mass media, film-making

08.02 Information science and policy

08.03 Library science and documentation

08.04 Computer science (incl. use of computers)

175

09.00 Transport

09.01 Transport (rural and urban) (general works)

09.02 Land transport

09.03 Water transport and harbours

09.04 Air transport
For transport equipment see resp. groups; for civil engineering works see 21.09.

10.00 Science, research and technology

10.01 Natural science, technology, engineering, research and development, research methods and theory (general works, directories, encyclopedias)

10.02 Transfer of technology (legal and fiscal aspects, patents)

10.03 Appropriate/alternative/applied technology (AT), traditional, intermediate technology, etc., economic and social aspect, directories
10.03.01 AT manuals (technical aspect)

10.04 Mathematics

10.05 Physics

10.06 Chemistry

10.07 Geology

10.08 Biology

10.09 Biotechnology, genetic engineering

11.00 Ecology, environment, natural resources

11.01 Natural resources, geography
    11.01.01 Climate, weather, meteorology

11.02 Ecology, environmental policy, eco-development studies

11.03 Resources conservation, environmental protection
    11.03.01 Arid zones, desertification
    11.03.02 Nature reserve, game reserve
    11.03.03 Rainforests and rainforest conservation

11.04 Erosion and erosion control
For techniques see agriculture and forestry.

11.05 Pollution and pollution control
    11.05.01 Air pollution
    11.05.02 Water pollution
    11.05.03 Soil pollution
    11.05.04 Others

11.06 Solid waste disposal

12.00 Water, sanitation and sewage disposal

12.01 Water and sanitation, hydrology

12.02 Water resources (surface water, groundwater)

12.03 Hydraulic structures (dams, intakes, wells, ponds, cisterns)

12.04 Pumps and other water-lifting devices
    12.04.01 Hand pumps
    12.04.02 Animal-powered pumps
    12.04.03 Motor-powered pumps
    12.04.04 Solar-powered pumps
    12.04.05 Wind-powered pumps
    12.04.06 Water-powered pumps
    12.04.07 Others

12.05 Water supply and storage

12.06 Water treatment (biological, chemical, physical)

12.07 Sanitation and sewage disposal
    12.07.01 Latrines (all kinds)
             For solid waste disposal see 11.06.

13.00 Health and nutrition

13.01 Health (general works, incl. health economics and sociology, health statistics, health and community development)

13.02 Health planning and policy, public health systems

13.03 Nutrition and malnutrition

13.04 Family health (incl. mother and child care, family planning)

13.05 Medical science, medical care, hygiene (treatment of specific diseases, injuries, accidents)

13.06 Methods of medical care
    13.06.01 "Western" medicine, allopathy
    13.06.02 Traditional and alternative methods (acupuncture, acupressure, homeopathy, etc.)

13.07 Production and use of medicines
    13.07.01 Pharmaceuticals
    13.07.02 Herbal medicines, medicinal plants

13.08 Health material and equipment

14.00 Agriculture and food processing

14.01 Agriculture (general works), agricultural economics, agricultural development, agricultural science and research, farm management
14.01.01 Land reform and related topics
14.01.02 Agricultural training

14.02 Agricultural production systems
(shifting cultivation, wet-land farming, dry-land farming, agro-forestry)

14.03 Organic farming, eco-farming

14.04 Agricultural implements, tools and machinery
(incl. mechanization, agricultural transport)
For implements specific to particular plants see respective plant.

14.05 Soil management and treatment
(incl. terracing, erosion control techniques)

14.06 Irrigation and drainage
For hydraulic structures see 12.03.

14.07 Fertilization and composting

14.08 Storage and packaging of agricultural products

14.09 Agricultural waste processing
For energy use see 20.06.

14.10 Food processing
14.10.01 Food preservation and storage
14.10.02 Food drying (all kinds)

15.00 Plant production and processing

15.01 Plant/crop production and processing, gardening, botany (general works and publications comprising several plants)

15.02 Plant protection (incl. insecticidinal plants)

15.03 Plant cultivation, seeds, seedbanks

15.04 Cereals (rice, corn/maize, millet, sorghum, wheat, etc.)

15.05 Starchy crops (cassava, potatoes, etc.)

15.06 Oil-producing plants, vegetable oil, nuts

15.07 Garden vegetables, legumes, mushrooms

15.08 Fruits and wine

15.09 Sugar-producing plants

15.10 Stimulants (coffee, tea, cocoa, coca, etc.)

15.11 Aromatic plants, dye plants, herbs and spices
For medicinal plants see 13.07.02.

15.12 Rubber, resin, wax plants

15.13 Textile and fibre plants
For processing see 19.08.

15.14 Fodder and pasture plants

15.15 Other plants/crops

16.00 Animal husbandry and animal product processing

16.01 Animal husbandry (general works) incl. animal feed and works covering several animals, zoology

16.02 Veterinary medicine, animal diseases

16.03 Animal traction (excl. implements), animal training

16.04 Horses, donkeys, mules

16.05 Cattle

16.06 Goats, sheep, camels

16.07 Pigs

16.08 Rabbits and guinea pigs

16.09 Poultry and other birds

16.10 Beekeeping and honey extraction

16.11 Other animals (silkworms, reptiles, frogs, snails, game, etc.)

16.12 Animal product processing
For processing of wool and silk see 19.08.
For processing of leather see 19.09.
   16.12.01 Meat processing and slaughtering
   16.12.02 Milk and egg processing (dairy, cheese)

17.00 Fishery and aquaculture

17.01 Fishery and aquaculture (general works), fishery resources

17.02 Fishing techniques and equipment
     17.02.01 Fishing gear (traditional and modern)
     17.02.02 Fishing boats

17.03 Fish farming, fish production (fish ponds, feeding, etc.)

17.04 Specific fishes, crustaceans, molluscs, etc.

17.05 Water plants and mangroves

17.06 Fishery product processing, storage, and marketing

17.07 Commercial fishing (economic and social aspect)

17.08 Small-scale fishing (economic and social aspect)

17.09 Fish diseases and control

18.00 Forestry

18.01 Forestry, general works

18.02 Reforestation
For erosion control see 11.04 and 14.05.

18.03 Cultivation and conservation (nurseries)

18.04 Forestry works

18.05 Specific trees and other forestry plants (incl. bamboo)

19.00 Industry, manufacture and services

19.01 Industry (general works, textbooks, directories)
incl. industrial planning

19.02 Industrial training, consulting
For vocational training see 07.08.

19.03 Small-scale industry, handicraft, home industry

19.04 Industrial profiles and studies covering several sectors

19.05 Recycling

19.06 Services industry (repair shops, hotels, laundries, travel agency, hairdresser, etc.)

19.07 Mining and quarrying

19.08 Textile industry, manufacture of wearing apparel
(incl. processing of natural fibres)

19.09 Leather industry

19.10 Wooden products and furniture

19.11 Pulp and paper products
(incl. printing and bookbinding)

19.12 Chemical and chemical products industry
incl. soap and candle production, salt

19.13 Pottery, ceramics, glass and glass products
(incl. jewellery, buttons, chalk)

19.14 Metal industry
    19.14.01 Forging and blacksmithing
    19.14.02 Manufacture and maintenance of cars, tractors, bicycles, motorcycles, ships and other transport equipment incl. resp. repair shops and training
    19.14.03 Manufacture of metal household equipment
               (incl. metal furniture)

19.15 Electrical and electronic industry
(incl. washing machines, refrigerators, etc.)

19.16 Instrumentation industry

19.17 Packaging industry

20.00 Energy

20.01 Energy and power (general works)
incl. energy per country, energy savings, and publications covering several sources of energy

20.02 Transformation, distribution and storage of energy
20.02.01 Rural electrification

20.03 Conventional energy resources (oil, petroleum, coal, natural gas, peat, nuclear energy)

20.04 Renewable energy resources
20.04.01 Bio-mass (general works)

20.05 Wood and charcoal (incl. kilns and activated charcoal)

20.06 Solid fuels from agricultural wastes and other organic material (pellets, eco-bricks, briquets)

20.07 Biogas (incl. biogas equipment)

20.08 Fuel-saving cookstoves

20.09 Wood gas, producer gas

20.10 Alcohol and other liquid fuels

20.11 Solar energy

20.12 Wind energy

20.13 Hydropower

21.00 Settlements, housing and construction

21.01 Settlements and housing: general works
incl. low-cost housing, planning techniques, surveying, etc.

21.02 Urban settlements (urban housing programmes, urbanization, squatters, slums, slum improvement)

21.03 Rural settlements

21.04 Building design, architecture
    21.04.01 Solar architecture

21.05 Construction materials

21.06 Building machinery

21.07 Housing construction (building components, construction techniques)

21.08 Technical services (installation works, plumbing, sanitary engineering) excl. hydraulic structures

21.09 Civil engineering (roads, bridges, etc.)

Alphabetical Index to Rural Development Classification

Cooperatives, consumer   03.09.05
Cooperatives, credit   03.09.02
Cooperatives, housing   03.09.04
Cooperatives, production
   03.09.03
Corn   15.04
Cost-benefit analysis   03.03
Cotton   15.13
Country reports   03.02
Credit   03.05.02
Credit cooperatives   03.09.02
Credit policy   03.05.02
Crop processing   15.00
Crop production   15.00
Crop rotation   14.03
Crustaceans   17.04
Cultivation of forests   18.03
Culture   06.00

Dairy products   16.12.02
Dams   12.03
Defence policy   05.05
Demography   06.06
Desertification   11.03.01
Deserts   11.03.01
Development   02.00
Development plan   02.02
Development planning   02.02
Development policy   02.01
Development theory   02.01
Dictionaries   01.02
Directories, general   01.01
Directories, specific, see subject
Disarmament   05.05
Diseases, treatment of   13.05
Dissemination strategies   02.03
Distribution of energy   20.02

Documentation   08.03
Donkeys   16.04
Drainage   14.06
Drugs   13.07
Dry-land farming   14.02
Drying of food products
   14.10.02
Dye plants   15.11
Dyeing of textiles   19.08

Earth-moving machinery   21.06
Eco-bricks   20.06
Eco-development studies   11.02
Eco-farming   14.03
Ecology   11.00/11.02
Economic analysis   03.03
Economic planning   03.03
Economic policy   03.02
Economic situation   03.02
Economic theory   03.01
Economics   03.00
Education   07.00/07.01
Education, higher   07.07
Education, primary   07.05
Education, secondary   07.06
Educational facilities   07.02
Egg processing   16.12.02
Electrical industry   19.15
Electrical installation   21.08
Electrification   20.02
Electrification, rural   20.02.01
Electronic industry   19.15
Employment generation strategy
   03.08.01
Employment policy   03.08.01
Encyclopedias, general   01.01
Encyclopedias, specific, see subject

Fur industry   19.09
Furniture, medical   13.08
Furniture, metal   19.14.03
Furniture, wooden   19.10

Game   16.11
Game reserve   11.03.02
Garbage   11.06
Garden vegetables   15.07
Gardening   15.01
Garment industry   19.08
Gas, methane   20.07
Gas, natural   20.03
Gas, producer   20.09
Gas, wood   20.09
General reference   01.00
Genetic engineering   10.09
Geography   11.01
Geology   10.07
Glass industry   19.13
Glass products   19.13
Glossaries   01.02
Goats   16.06
Gobar gas   20.07
Government   05.01
Groundwater   12.02
Guinea pigs   16.08

Hairdresser   19.06
Hand pumps   12.04.01
Handicraft   19.03
Harbours   09.03
Health   13.00
Health and community development   13.01
Health economics   13.01
Health equipment   13.08

Health material   13.08
Health planning   13.02
Health policy   13.02
Health sociology   13.01
Health statistics   13.01
Herbal medicines   13.07.02
Herbs   15.11
Higher education   07.07
Hinduism   06.11.03
History   06.08
Home industry   19.03
Homeopathy   13.06.02
Honey extraction   16.10
Horses   16.04
Hotels   19.06
Housing   21.00
Housing construction   21.07
Housing cooperatives   03.09.04
Human rights   05.04
Human rights violation   05.04
Hydraulic rams   12.04
Hydraulic structures   12.03
Hydroelectricity   20.13
Hydrology   12.01
Hydropower   20.13
Hygiene   13.05

Import   03.06
Industrial development   03.04
Industrial economics   03.04
Industrial free zones   03.04
Industrial planning   19.01
Industrial profiles   19.04
Industrial training   19.02
Industrialization   03.04
Industrialization, rural   03.04
Industry   19.00

Metal-working techniques   19.14
Meteorology   11.01.01
Methane gas   20.07
Military   05.05
Milk processing   16.12.02
Millet   15.04
Mining   19.07
Minorities   06.03
MNC   03.04
Molluscs   17.04
Monetary economics   03.05
Mother and child care   13.04
Motor   20.02
Motor-powered pumps   12.04.03
Motor vehicle repair shop
  19.14.02
Motorcycle   19.14.02
Mud and earth   21.05
Mud block presses   21.06
Mules   16.04
Multinational corporations   03.04
Municipal fishing   17.08
Mushrooms   15.07
Music   06.12

National organizations   02.06.03
National plan   02.02
National planning   02.02
National statistical yearbooks
  03.02
Natural gas   20.03
Natural resources   11.00/11.01
Natural science   10.01
Nature reserve   11.03.02
NGO   02.05
Nongovernmental organization
  02.05

Nuclear energy   20.03
Nutrition   13.03
Nuts   15.06

Office management   04.04
Oil   20.03
Oil palm   15.06
Oil-producing plants   15.06
Optical instruments   19.16
Organic farming   14.03
Organizations, international
  02.06.01
Organizations, national   02.06.03
Organizations, regional   02.06.02
Organizations, social   06.02
Organizations, voluntary   02.05

Packaging industry   19.17
Packaging of agricultural products
  14.08
Paper   19.11
Participatory research   06.01
Participatory training   06.01
Pasture plants   15.14
Peace movements   05.05
Peasant movements   06.03
Peasant organizations   06.03
Peat   20.03
Pellets   20.06
Personnel management   04.03
Pest control   15.02
Pesticides   15.02
Petrol   20.03
Pharmaceuticals   13.07.01
Philosophy   06.07
Physics   10.05
Pigs   16.07

Statistics   04.07
Stimulants   15.10
Stone (construction material)
   21.05
Storage of agricultural products
   14.08
Storage of energy   20.02
Storage of fishery products   17.06
Storage of food   14.10.01
Sugar-producing plants   15.09
Surface water   12.02
Surveying   21.01

Tanning   19.09
Tea   15.10
Teaching aids   07.03
Teaching method   07.03
Technical services   21.08
Technology   10.00/10.01
Technology, alternative   10.03
Technology, applied   10.03
Technology, appropriate   10.03
Technology, intermediate   10.03
Technology, traditional   10.03
Technology, transfer of   10.02
Telecommunication   08.01
Terminology   01.02
Terracing   14.05
Textile finishing   19.08
Textile industry   19.08
Textile plants   15.13
Textile printing   19.08
Theatre   06.12
Theology   06.11.02
Thesaurus   08.03
Timber production   19.10
TNC   03.04

Tourism   03.07
Tractor   19.14.02
Trade   03.06
Trade unionism   03.08.02
Trade unions   03.08.02
Traditional medicine   13.06.02
Traditional technology   10.03
Training   07.00/07.01
Training, vocational   07.08
Training centres   07.02
Transfer of technology   10.02
Transformation of energy   20.02
Transnational corporations   03.04
Transport   09.00/09.01
Transport, agricultural   14.04
Transport, rural   09.01
Transport, urban   09.01
Transport equipment, manufacture
   of   19.14.02
Travel agency   19.06
Treatment of specific diseases
   13.05
Tree   18.05

Universities   07.07
Upholstery   19.10
Urban housing programmes
   21.02
Urban settlements   21.02
Urban transport   09.01
Urbanization   21.02

Vegetable oil   15.06
Vegetables   15.07
Veterinary medicine   16.02
Vocational training   07.08
Voluntary organizations   02.05

Washing machines   19.15
Waste disposal, solid   11.06
Waste processing, agricultural
   14.09
Water   12.00
Water and sanitation   12.01
Water plants   17.05
Water pollution   11.05.02
Water-powered pumps   12.04
Water resources   12.02
Water storage   12.05
Water supply   12.05
Water supply systems   12.05
Water tanks   12.03
Water testing   12.06
Water transport   09.03
Water treatment   12.06
Water turbines   20.13
Water wheels   20.13
Wax plants   15.12
Wearing apparel, manufacture of
   19.08
Weather   11.01.01
Weaving   19.08
Weed control   15.02

Welfare   06.03
Wells   12.03
Western medicine   13.06.01
Wet-land farming   14.02
Wheat   15.04
Wild animals   16.11
Wind energy   20.12
Wind generators   20.12
Wind-powered pumps   12.04
Windmills   20.12
Wine   15.08
Women and development   06.04
Women's organizations   06.04
Wood (energy)   20.05
Wood carving   19.10
Wood drying   19.10
Wood gas   20.09
Wood-processing industry   19.10
Wooden products   19.10

Yams   15.05
Youth   06.05
Youth centres   06.05

Zoology   16.01

Annex II:
Additional Information on the Treatment of Authors' Names

The following extract is taken from the "Manual for the preparation of records in development-information systems" (by Gisèle Morin-Labatut and Maureen Sly. Ottawa: IDRC 1982. pages 50-57) and gives additional information on the treatment of names of personal authors in various regions and languages.

African names

For the following countries, the first name is the more significant element. Enter the full name exactly as it is found on the documentary unit.

Country	Examples
Chad	Sou Ngonn Sou
	Bongbanda Hogra
Ethiopia	Tesfa-Yesus Mehary
	Eshetu Habte Georgis
Madagascar	Razafindramainty
Mauritania	Moktar Ould Haiba
	Ahmed Ould Djeddou
Zaire	Ilanga Nyonschi
	Lumpungu Kamanda

Arabic names

1. When an Arabic name has only two elements, the second element is the family name.

Examples

Fatimah Barakat
B210: Barakat, Fatimah

Jamil Mattar
B210: Mattar, Jamil

2. Compound names containing prefixes

The prefixes Al, El, Abou, Abun, Abdul, Abdel, Ben, or Ibn are the first element of a compound name (family name or given name).

Examples

Mohammed Al-Afghani
B210: Al-Afghani, Mohammed

Tariq Ben Hamoud
B210: Ben Hamoud, Tariq

Tahir Abdul Hakim
B210: Abdul Hakim, Tahir

Abdel Khader Shukrallah
B210: Shukrallah, Abdel Khader

Tawfiq Abou Shakra
B210: Abou Shakra, Tawfiq

N. El-Madji-Amor
B210: El-Madji-Amor, N.

Abdul Rahman Ibn Khaldoun
B210: Ibn Khaldoun, Abdul Rahman

3. Compound names containing suffixes

"El-Dine" in its various forms ("al-din", "al-Din", etc.) is a suffix and therefore is always the second part of a compound name (family name or given name).

Examples

Ahmad Izz El-Dine
B210: Izz El-Dine, Ahmad

Kheir El-Dine Raouf
B210: Raouf, Kheir El-Dine

Muhammad Sadr al-Din
B210: Sadr al-Din, Muhammad

Asian names

Note: For Chinese and Korean names, see the section below on Chinese names.
When it is not possible to identify the family name(s) of an author, select the last element as the family name, as in the examples below.
Exception: Malaysian and Thai names are entered in the order in which they appear on the documentary unit.

Country	Examples
India	Chatterjee, Bishwa B. Sharma, Baldev Raj
Indonesia	Soedjatmoko Martadihardja Dachlan, Eddie Sumardi
Malaysia	Merican Faridah Abdullah Sanusi bin Ahmad
Pakistan	Siddiqui, Akhtar H. Hasnain, Mehdi
Thailand	Chakrit Noranitpadungkarn Jingjai Hanchanlash

Chinese names

Note: The following guidelines also apply to Korean names (see 6 below for examples of Korean names).

1. When a Chinese name has no Western element, it traditionally comprises a one-syllable family name followed by one or two given names. Enter such names exactly as they appear on the documentary unit, without adding any punctuation.

Examples

Lim Hong-Too
B210: Lim Hong-Too

Chung Ling
B210: Chung Ling

Mao Zedong
B210: Mao Zedong

2. People of Chinese origin living overseas, or Chinese writing for a Western audience, may write their given name(s) first, followed by the family name. If this can be ascertained, enter the family name first, followed by the given name(s).

Examples

Hwa-Wei Lee
B210: Lee Hwa-Wei

Yok-Leng Chan
B210: Chan Yok-Leng

3. Treat a name consisting of only a Western given name and a Chinese family name as a Western name.

Example

Richard Lee
B210: Lee, Richard

4. Enter a name consisting of a Western given name, a Chinese family name, and one or more Chinese given names, as in the examples below.

Examples

Philip Loh Fook Seng
B210: Loh, Philip Fook Seng

Maria Ng Lee Hoon
B210: Ng, Maria Lee Hoon

5. In case of doubt, copy the full name exactly as it appears on the documentary unit, without inserting any punctuation.

Example

Lim Huck Tee
B210: Lim Huck Tee

6. Korean names are entered according to the guidelines for Chinese names.

Examples

B210: Koh Hoe-Young
B210: Choe Jung-Tai
B210: Yu Kyong-Hee

B210: Lee Jai-Chuel
B210: Kim Ku
B210: Namgung Pyok

European names

Note: For Portuguese names, see the separate section below.

1. Compound family names

When a family name is hyphenated or known to be compound, treat it as one element; do not separate it.

Examples

T. Müller-Debus
B210: Müller-Debus, T.

W. Schneider-Barthold
B210: Schneider-Barthold, W.

Rita Cruise O'Brien
B210: Cruise O'Brien, Rita

Martha Beya de Modernell
B210: Beya de Modernell, Martha

Alfonso Medina Echeverría
B210: Medina Echeverría, Alfonso

C.L. Torres y Torres
B210: Torres y Torres, C.L.

Frederic Strickland-Constable
B210: Strickland-Constable, Frederic

2. Compound family names with prefix(es)

2.1 Enter the following prefixes after the given names:

af	op de	ter	**van der**	**von der**
den	ten	van	von	

Examples

P. von Blanckenburg
B210: Blanckenburg, P. von

M.P. van Dijk
B210: Dijk, M.P. van

Leo op de Beech
B210: Beech, Leo op de

Menno ter Braak
B210: Braak, Menno ter

Gunnar af Hallstrom
B210: Hallstrom, Gunnar af

2.2 Enter the following prefixes without inversion, i.e., before the family name:

am	del	di	la	les	ver	zur
de	della	du	las	li	vom	
de la	delle	l'	le	los	zum	

Examples

S.J. Du Toit
B210: Du Toit, S.J.

Jean de Chantal
B210: de Chantal, Jean

René La Bruyère
B210: La Bruyère, René

M. della Rosa
B210: della Rosa, M.

Isidoro del Lungo
B210: del Lungo, Isidoro

Bernardo la Fuente
B210: la Fuente, Bernardo

Susana las Heras
B210: las Heras, Susana

Aja ver Boven
B210: ver Boven, Aja

3. Portuguese names

3.1 Enter Portuguese names under the last element of the family name.

Examples

Ovidio Saraiva de Carvalho e Silva
B210: Silva, Ovidio Saraiva de Carvalho e

Paulo Fernando de Moraes Farias
B210: Farias, Paulo Fernando de Moraes

3.2 When the last element of the family name is a qualifier indicating a family relationship such as Júnior, Filho, Neto, Sobrinho, the qualifier is treated as a suffix in a compound name.

Examples

Victor Vidal Neto
B210: Vidal Neto, Victor

A.F. Coimbra Filho
B210: Coimbra Filho, A.F.

António Ribeiro de Castro Sobrinho
B210: Castro Sobrinho, António Ribeiro de

3.3 In former Portuguese colonies, the qualifier (Júnior, Filho, Neto, Sobrinho) sometimes constitutes the family name.

Examples

António Luís Neto
B210: Neto, António Luís

Jorge Sobrinho
B210: Sobrinho, Jorge

Index

(Page numbers printed in **bold type** refer to the glossary.)